PROSPERITY EDUCATION

WORK IT OUT

WITH BUSINESS IDIOMS

TEACHING RESOURCE
B2–C1

DAVID BOHLKE

PROSPERITY EDUCATION

Registered offices: Sherlock Close, Cambridge
CB3 0HP, United Kingdom

© Prosperity Education Ltd. 2021

First published 2021

ISBN: 978-1-913825-34-8

This publication is in copyright. Subject to statutory exception and to the provisions of relevant collective licensing agreements, no reproduction of any part may take place without the written permission of Prosperity Education.

The moral rights of the author have been asserted.

Typeset and produced by ORP Cambridge

Cover design by Frill Creative www.frillcreative.com

For further information and resources, visit:
www.prosperityeducation.net

To infinity and beyond.

Contents

About this book	1
Introduction	2
Work out 1: Meetings	4
Work out 2: Soft skills	9
Work out 3: Communication	13
Work out 4: Presentations	19
Work out 5: Teamwork	23
Work out 6: Sales and marketing	28
Work out 7: Problem-solving	33
Work out 8: Global branding	38
Work out 9: Customer relations	42
Work out 10: Corporate Social Responsibility	48
Work out 11: Leadership	54
Work out 12: Job interviews	60
Teaching tools	67
Handouts	85
Idiom dictionary	133
Download code	157

About this book

Work It Out with Business Idioms

Designed for both new and experienced teachers, *Work It Out with Business Idioms* is uniquely focused on presenting and practising idioms in a business or work-related context. With its highly communicative, student-centred approach, *Work It Out with Business Idioms* offers downloadable and photocopiable lesson materials, extensive teaching notes and a variety of inclusive activities for B2–C1 level students.

Key features

- Detailed lesson plans to ensure clear and effective delivery, from start to finish, including lead-ins and activities for practice, production, extension and review
- Activities and lesson adaptations to accommodate the needs of mixed-ability classes, and discussion questions to encourage critical thinking
- Digital lesson alternatives and online-teaching tips to support a blended-learning environment
- Extension exercises for more-confident students and activities for fast finishers

Downloadable and photocopiable content

- Teaching tools
- Handouts
- Idiom dictionary

Accompanying resources available from www.prosperityeducation.net

- Student workbook (class sets available; individual copies available on Amazon)
- eBook: the content of this print edition in pdf

About the author

David Bohlke is an ELT author, editor, trainer and consultant with 35 years of expertise in creating market-driven publishing materials. He has commissioned, edited and written some of the world's top-selling courses and skills texts for the adult, secondary and academic English markets, including: *Four Corners* and *Final Draft* (Cambridge University Press); *Keynote* and *Reading Explorer* (National Geographic Learning); *Skillful* (Macmillan Education); *Next Generation Grammar* (Pearson); and *Speak Now* (Oxford University Press).

Introduction

Preparing to work it out

Idioms exist in every language. They are common in both written and spoken texts. It's a no-brainer that your English will sound better if you are able to recognise and understand idioms successfully. But in the past, did you have to rack your brains trying to learn idioms? Did they go in one ear and then out the other? Did you use an idiom incorrectly, resulting in having egg on your face? Learning idioms is no piece of cake, but this resource can help you from the get-go!

To make the most of the activities in this book and to maximise students' learning, you may wish to read this introductory section when using *Work It Out with Business Idioms* for the first time.

Work It Out with Business Idioms comprises:

- lesson themes that fit with common business English coursebooks
- 96 business idioms presented in both written and spoken contexts
- adaptable lessons to meet the unique needs of each class
- a dictionary with real-world examples

As classes come in all abilities and sizes, each unit offers a number of features:

- step-by-step teaching instructions
- adaptations for less-confident students
- activities for fast finishers
- extension and variation activities
- expected timings for each activity
- digital tips
- activities and games for review
- handouts and answer keys

Each of the twelve units is called a *Work out* and these can be worked through sequentially or used as standalone lessons.

What exactly is an idiom?
An idiom is a group of words whose collective meaning is not apparent from the meaning of its individual words. There is often more than meets the eye because an idiom's meaning is typically figurative, not literal. For example, you know what the individual words mean in the idiom 'hit the nail on the head'. However, you are not physically hitting a nail. Its meaning – to describe exactly what's causing a situation or problem – is not obvious from the words themselves.

How can I understand idioms?
You may recognise an idiom as you read and listen to English, but *recognising* an idiom is just half the battle. How do you actually understand its *meaning*? A good rule of thumb is that, once you recognise an idiom, you should look for context clues.

These are words that appear before or after the idiom in the sentence or in neighbouring sentences. There are several different types of context clues to look for:

Definition clues
There may be words before or after the idiom that essentially define the idiom.

- Aggressive communicators are honest. They like to 'tell it like it is' and **put their cards on the table** for all to see and hear.

If you 'put your cards on the table', you talk openly about your feelings and intentions. This is another way of saying you are being honest (and telling it like it is).

- It can **cost a corporation an arm and a leg** to be socially responsible. These additional expenses can lead to increased costs for the customer.

If something costs 'an arm and a leg', it's very expensive. The second sentence (these additional expenses … increased costs for the customer) helps define the idiom.

Example clues
There may be words before or after the idiom that provide an example of what the idiom is describing.

- He tends to **go with the flow**. He ensures that everything goes smoothly by being an active listener and task facilitator.

If someone 'goes with the flow', they do what everyone else is doing. A good example of this is being an active listener and task facilitator.

- Other types of skills are gained through personal relationships and **learning the ropes** through on-the-job experience.

When you 'learn the ropes', you learn how to do a task or job. On-the-job experience is one way of achieving this.

Comparison and contrast clues
There may be words before or after the idiom that make a comparison or a contrast.

- But if we look closely, we can see that sales remain steady in Europe and the Middle East. In the Americas, they've **gone through the roof**. Yet sales are way down in Asia.

Sales that have gone 'through the roof' have risen to a very high level. The sales in the Americas are compared to and contrasted with steady sales in Europe and the Middle East, and lower sales in Asia.

- It's time to decide on one solution. This is **a piece of cake** for some people, but others struggle to make a firm decision.

If a decision is 'a piece of cake', it's a very easy task. The opposite is true for those who struggle to make a firm decision.

I hope that this resource proves to be a useful companion to you as you help your students to **get ahead of the curve**!

David Bohlke

Work out **1**

Meetings

The amount of time an employee spends in meetings has increased every year since 2008. – Bain & Co.

B2+

Resources	Handout 1.1	one copy per pair
	Handout 1.2	one copy per pair
	Handout 1.3	one copy per pair
	Handout 1.4	one copy per pair
	Teaching tool 1.1	one copy per group

Target language

Beat (someone) to the punch – to achieve something before someone else does

Get down to business – to start working

Get (someone) up to speed – to give someone all the information they need

Have a lot on one's plate – to have many things to do

Have money to burn – to have more money than one needs

Not going to fly – not going to work well

Up and running – operating normally

Work around the clock – to work all day and all night (to get the job done)

1
- Write the following questions on the board:

  How often do you take part in face-to-face meetings? In online meetings?

  What do you like and dislike about meetings? Why?

  How did you contribute to the last meeting you attended?

- Put students in small groups to discuss the questions.
- Elicit ideas from the class.

5–10 mins

2
- Have students work in pairs.
- Give each pair a copy of the cut-up conversation in **Handout 1.1**.

10–15 mins

Work out 1: Meetings

- Ask the class:

  How many people are participating in the meeting? (four)

  Is the meeting face-to-face or online? (online)

  Who is running the meeting? (Martin)

  What section is the first part of the conversation? (F)

- Ask students to underline the idioms they find.

- Have students put the rest of the conversation strips in order. Monitor and provide support as needed.

- Elicit answers by asking a pair to read their ordered conversation. Other pairs should check that they have the same order.

Extra support
If students have difficulty identifying the idioms in the conversation, provide hints by saying one word from each idiom (e.g. *business, plate, speed, money, beat, working, fly, up*).

Fast finishers
As pairs finish, ask them to extend the conversation by adding another turn by one of the speakers.

Answer key Handout 1.1	1 F 2 B 3 H 4 D 5 C 6 I 7 E 8 A 9 G

3

- Give each pair a copy of **Handout 1.2**. Have the class look at the first question. Ask:

15–20 mins

  After the introductions, who suggests that they start working? (Martin)

- Tell students they can refer to Handout 1.1 to help them find the answers.

- Ask them to write their answers in the *Answers* column of Handout 1.2.

- Have students look at Handout 1.1 again. Ask which words helped them to answer Question 1.

- Elicit the answer to Question 1 (*let's get down to business*).

- Have students write the words that helped them in the *Which words...?* column of Handout 1.2.

Work It Out with Business Idioms

- o   If necessary, go over the second question as a class.
- o   Ask pairs to answer the rest of the questions.
- o   Elicit answers.

Answer key		Questions	Answers	Which words...?
Handout 1.2	1	After the introductions, who suggests that they start working?	Martin	...let's get down to business.
	2	Does Martin think that Paula and Lukas have little to do these days?	no	...you all have a lot on your plate...
	3	Does Martin quickly get Paula and Lukas all the information they need?	yes	Let me quickly get everyone up to speed...
	4	Do their competitors probably have more or less money than they need?	more	...seem to have money to burn...
	5	Does Martin want to achieve something before or after their competitors do?	before	...we beat them to the punch.
	6	Have Paula and Lukas been working day and night to make the launch happen?	yes	...all been working around the clock...
	7	Does Paula think that a spring launch is going to work for her?	no	...don't think spring is going to fly...
	8	How much time does Paula need for the launch to start operating normally?	until summer	...need until the summer to get everything up and running...

4
- o   Give each pair a copy of **Handout 1.3**.
- o   Ask the pairs to complete Samantha's notes with the words in the box. Remind them that two words are extra and are not used.

15–20 mins

Work out 1: Meetings

- o Tell students to look at Handout 1.1 to help them find the answers.
- o Elicit answers.

Answer key	1 business	2 plate	3 speed	4 burn
Handout 1.3	5 beat	6 clock	7 fly	8 up

5
- o Give each pair a copy of **Handout 1.4**.
- o Ask students to match the beginning and end of each question.
- o Elicit answers.
- o Have each pair join another pair to make a small group.
- o Tell groups to discuss each question. Encourage them to ask follow-up questions to get more information.

20–25 mins

Extension activity
Have one or two students share any interesting answers they heard in their discussions.

Answer key								
Handout 1.4	1 b	2 d	3 g	4 f	5 a	6 c	7 h	8 e

6
- o Before class starts, copy **Teaching tool 1.1** for each group. Cut into 16 cards: 8 idioms; 8 definitions.
- o Divide the class into groups of three or four. Give each group a set of 16 cards.
- o Tell groups to keep the idiom cards in one pile and the definition cards in another. Place both sets of cards face down, side by side.
- o A volunteer from each group turns over the top card in the idioms pile. They then turn over the top card from the definitions pile. The two cards are left face up so each group member can see them.
- o If the two cards match (idiom + definition), the students slap the table with one hand as quickly as possible. The first person to slap the table then takes the two cards. If the two cards are not a match, anyone who slapped the table must sit out the next turn. Tell students to ask you, if they are unsure whether there is a match.
- o The next player takes a turn. Once all the cards are face up, shuffle each pile of cards and put them face down, and continue playing.

15–20 mins

o   Continue until all the cards are removed. The player with the most pairs is the winner.

> **Extra challenge**
> Tell students to make a sentence with the idiom after they find a matching pair. If the sentence does not make sense or shows that the student does not understand the meaning of the idiom, the student loses a turn and must put the cards back in their place.

Work out 2

Soft skills

Talents without skills is like deserts without an oasis. – Islamic proverb

B2+

Resources	Handout 2.1	one copy per group
	Handout 2.2	one copy per pair
	Handout 2.3	one copy per pair
	Teaching tool 2.1	one copy per group
	Teaching tool 2.2	one copy per class

Target language

A rule of thumb – a principle that is based on experience

Half the battle – a significant part of the work that is needed

In a nutshell – in only a few words

Learn the ropes – to learn how to do a task or job

Push (someone) over the finish line – to make a final effort towards a goal

Step up to the plate – to take responsibility for doing something difficult or unpopular

The bottom line – the most important fact in a situation

Tick all the boxes – to meet all the requirements

1
- Write the following questions on the board:

  What are some important skills to have in business?

  Which skills used to be important, but are less so now? Why?

  What might be some business-important skills in the future? Why?

- Put students in small groups to discuss the questions.
- Elicit ideas from the class.

5–10 mins

2
- Before class starts, cut up **Teaching tool 2.1** into the three parts. Prepare one part (A, B or C) for each student.
- Tell the class that they are going to work together to understand a text about soft skills.

30–40 mins

Work It Out with Business Idioms

- o Divide the class into three 'expert' groups: Group A, Group B and Group C.

- o Give each student in Group A a copy of the A text. Give each student in Group B the B text, and each student in Group C the C text. Explain that each group has only one-third of the whole text at this time.

- o Have each of the three 'expert' groups study their part together to ensure that everyone in their group understands it.

- o Explain that each student has to understand their part well because they will later have to share and explain the information.

- o Ask students to guess the meaning of any idioms they find, and to share their ideas within their group. Do not allow them to use dictionaries.

- o When you feel that the students have become 'experts' in their part of the text, have them create a new 'cooperative group' of three different students, with one A student, one B student and one C student. As a group, they now have the whole text, but each student still has only one-third of it.

- o Ask the students in each 'cooperative' group to now take turns to share orally what their part of the text says.

- o Discourage them from simply reading their part of the text aloud. Instead, they should summarise their text.

- o If they don't understand something in another group member's text, encourage them to ask for repetition or ask questions to get further clarification.

- o When you feel that each 'cooperative' group has a good understanding of the whole text, give each student a copy of **Handout 2.1**. Tell them to discuss the six questions as a group and write their answers.

- o Monitor and assist as needed. When most groups have finished, elicit answers.

- o Provide each student with a copy of the complete text from Teaching tool 2.1.

> Extra support
>
> While students are trying to understand their part of the text, they may have questions about the meaning of words or idioms. To encourage peer teaching, have them ask their group members for help. If no one knows, they can ask you.

Work out 2: Soft skills

Answer key		Questions	Answers
Handout 2.1	1	What are two examples of 'hard skills'?	o speaking a foreign language o using a certain software programme
	2	What's another name for 'soft skills'?	o people skills
	3	What are three examples of soft skills?	o how well we motivate others o how well we work as part of a team o using time effectively o stepping up the plate when needed o building trust
	4	What's one way to identify your soft skills?	o ask yourself if someone has ever praised you for something that involved using a soft skill o think about what soft skills may have helped you with success at work
	5	Which types of skills do employers look for?	o both hard and soft skills
	6	What does 'transferable skills' mean?	o you can take and use the skills elsewhere

3

- o Have students work in pairs.

- o Ask them to look again at their complete text (A–C). Have them find and underline the eight idioms in the text.

- o Elicit answers, but do not go over the meanings.

- o Give each pair a copy of **Handout 2.2**. Ask students to check that the idioms they underlined in the text are the same as the ones in Handout 2.2.

- o Have them circle the meaning (a or b) of each underlined idiom.

- o Elicit answers.

15–20 mins

Digital tip
Have students search online for the types of skills employers are looking for in their new employees these days. Have them divide the skills into hard skills and soft skills.

Answer key Handout 2.2	1 a 2 b 3 a 4 b 5 b 6 b 7 a 8 a

Work It Out with Business Idioms

4
- Give each pair a copy of **Handout 2.3**.
- Ask the pairs to complete the questions with the words in the box. Remind them that two words are extra and are not used.
- Tell students to look at Teaching tool 2.1 to help them find the answers.
- Elicit answers.
- Have pairs join another pair. Ask them to discuss each question. Tell them that each student should answer each question.

15–20 mins

Answer key	1 nutshell	2 half	3 rule	4 ropes
Handout 2.3	5 ticks	6 push	7 plate	8 bottom

5
- Before class starts, copy **Teaching tool 2.2**. Cut into cards and place each set of eight cards, in two piles, face down in front of the board.
- Divide the class into two groups: Team 1 and Team 2.
- One volunteer student from each team stands at the board. Each volunteer picks up an idiom card from their team's pile and draws a picture of it on the board. The students who are drawing cannot talk, use gestures or include words or letters in the drawings.
- If a student's teammates can correctly guess the idiom within 30 seconds, the team gets a point.
- If no one guesses correctly from the team within 30 seconds, the other teams get *one* guess and can 'steal' the point.
- It's possible for both teams to get a point, or one team to get a point, or neither team to get a point.
- Continue the game with two new volunteers picking two more cards. When the cards are finished, shuffle them and continue, as time allows. The team with the most points at the end of the time wins.

10–15 mins

> **Extra challenge**
> If you have taught more idioms than the ones on the cards, consider reviewing these as well. Create cards with the additional idioms and include them in the pile.

Work out 3

Communication

Wise men speak because they have something to say;
Fools because they have to say something. – Plato

B2+

Resources	Handout 3.1	one copy per pair
	Handout 3.2	one copy per student
	Handout 3.3	one copy per student
	Teaching tool 3.1	one copy per class/student

Target language

At the drop of a hat – immediately and without delay

Get a word in edgeways – to have a chance to speak

Get one's point across – to make something clear to someone

Get the short end of the stick – to suffer the bad effects of a situation

Give (someone) a hand – to give someone assistance

In one ear and out the other – forgotten immediately after being heard

Meet (someone) halfway – to compromise with someone

Put one's cards on the table – to talk openly about one's feelings and intentions

---

1

o Have students sit in a large circle. If you have a class of more than 10 students, you may want to have two circles.

5–10 mins

o Say that you are going to whisper a sentence in one student's ear. Choose one of the following sentences:

I am ready to help you out at the drop of a hat.

If you can't do what I want, try to meet me halfway.

For some reason I always seem to get the short end of the stick.

Many people were talking at once so I couldn't get a word in edgeways.

I have no idea what you said because it went in one ear and out the other.

o That student then whispers what they've heard to the person on their right. That student then whispers what they've heard to the person on their right, and so on.

- Tell students that they are not allowed to write the sentence down or take notes, but they can ask for repetition before they share it with the next student.
- Continue until the sentence has reached the last student in the circle.
- Ask the last student to say what they heard, or have them write it on the board. Compare it with the original sentence. It will probably be very different from the original sentence.
- Ask students if they can identify the idiom in the sentence.
- Repeat the activity with another sentence, as time allows.

> Extension activity
>
> When you whisper a sentence into one student's ear, have them tell the person to their right. At the same time, whisper a different sentence into another student's ear. Have them whisper it to the person on their *left*. You now have two sentences going into different directions. Check the sentences after they make a full circle.

2
- Before class starts, cut up **Teaching tool 3.1** into four parts. Tape each part to the wall in four different corners of the room.

15–20 mins

- Ask students to think about how they communicate with others. Ask if they have ever thought about what their communication style might be.
- Ask students to stand up and walk to each corner of the room and read about the different communication styles on the walls. Tell them there is no correct order, so they can start with any corner they wish.
- After they've read each of the four styles, ask students which style they think applies to them. Have them stand in that corner.
- When all students have chosen their styles, write these questions on the board, for students to discuss with the other students in their corner:

Why did you choose this communication style?

Do you think your communication style changes depending on the situation you're in? Explain.

What kind of style would you like your coworkers or boss to have? Why?

- After the discussion, ask students to return to their seats.

Work out 3: Communication

3
- Have students work in pairs.
- Give each student a copy of **Teaching tool 3.1**.

15–20 mins

- Ask students to underline the idioms they find.
- Give each pair a copy of **Handout 3.1**. Have the class look at the first question. Ask:

What do Passive Communicators do when they're asked to help others? (say 'yes')

- Tell students to look at Teaching tool 3.1 to help them find the answers.
- Ask them to write their answers in the *Answers* column of Handout 3.1.
- Have students look at Handout 3.1 again. Ask which words helped them to answer Question 1.
- Elicit the answer (*give someone a hand*).
- Have students write the words that helped them in the *Which words…?* column of Handout 3.1.
- If necessary, go over the second question as a class.
- Ask pairs to answer the rest of the questions.
- Elicit answers.

Answer key		Questions	Answers	Which words…?
Handout 3.1	1	What do Passive Communicators do when they're asked to help others?	say 'yes'	…give someone a hand.
	2	Do Passive Communicators tend to suffer the bad effects of a situation?	yes	…get the short end of the stick.
	3	Are Aggressive Communicators open or closed about their feelings and intentions?	open	…put their cards on the table…
	4	Do people have a chance to speak when they listen to Aggressive Communicators?	no	…hard to get a word in edgeways.

	5	Do people hear and remember all that Passive-aggressive Communicators say?	no	...go in one ear and out the other.
	6	Do Passive-aggressive Communicators use humour to make what they say clear?	yes	...get their point across...
	7	Do Assertive Communicators tend to compromise with others?	yes	...quick to meet people halfway.
	8	Do Assertive Communicators help others right away, or after some time has passed?	right away	...help others at the drop of a hat.

4

20–25 mins

- Give each student a copy of **Handout 3.2**.
- Ask students to stand up and mingle with the class. Tell them that they will need to find different people who answer 'yes' to each question.
- If necessary, go over how to form the questions for the first one or two questions (*Do you get embarrassed at the drop of a hat? Are you happy to give another student a hand with their homework?*)
- If a student answers 'yes' to a question, the student asking the question should write down the other student's name and ask a follow-up question to get more information. Tell them to take notes on the responses. If someone answers 'no', the student can either move on or ask a different question.
- When students have completed the table, they can return in their seats.
- Stop the activity when most of the students have completed the table.
- Elicit any interesting information the students have learned about their classmates.

Work out 3: Communication

5

20–25 mins

- Have students work in pairs.
- Give each student a copy of **Handout 3.3**.
- Ask students to look through the questions and possible answers. Go over any unfamiliar vocabulary.
- Tell them that they are going to find out what communication style they have.
- Have each student quiz their partner by taking turns to ask the questions (1–9) and stating the four possible responses (a–d). Ask them to circle the letter (a–d) of their partner's responses.
- After they have completed the quiz, tell students to count the number of a, b, c and d responses. Have them write the number of responses for each letter at the bottom of Handout 3.3.
- Share the following information orally with the class, or write it on the board.

  Mostly a answers = Passive Communicator

  Mostly b answers = Aggressive Communicator

  Mostly c answers = Passive-aggressive Communicator

  Mostly d answers = Assertive Communicator

- Ask students whether they agree with the quiz results. Ask them if the results match the communication style they stood next to earlier.

> Extension activity
> Ask students to guess your communication style. Ask them for reasons before sharing what style you are.

6

10–15 mins

- Have students work in pairs.
- Ask students to work together to write a conversation between a boss and an employee. The conversation should be between six and eight lines in length.
- Tell students that the conversation should show two of the four communication styles – one for the boss and one for the employee. They can choose any situation they like.
- Insist that each pair should include in their conversation at least one of the idioms they have learned.
- Give a time limit of five or so minutes. Monitor and provide support as needed.

Work It Out with Business Idioms

- o When they are finished, ask one pair to come to the front of the class to read and act out their conversation. The other students guess the communication style of each person.

- o Ask other pairs to read or act out their conversation for the class as time allows.

Work out 4

Presentations

'If you can't explain it simply, you don't understand it well enough.'
– Albert Einstein

B2+

Resources	Handout 4.1	one copy per student
	Handout 4.2	one copy, as required
	Handout 4.3	one copy, as required
	Handout 4.4	one copy, as required
	Handout 4.5	one copy, as required
	Teaching tool 4.1	one copy per group of four

Target language

A no-brainer – something that is very obvious

Beat around the bush – to avoid or delay talking about something

Cut to the chase – to get directly to the main point

Do something with one's eyes closed – to do something very easily

Fall on deaf ears – to be ignored by someone

Go overboard – to do something too much

In the market for something – interested in buying something

Put one's best foot forward – to make the best possible impression

---

1
- Write the following questions on the board:

    What makes a great presentation?

    Do you ever give presentations as part of your job? To whom?

    What do you think an 'elevator pitch' is?

- Put students in small groups to discuss the questions.

- Elicit ideas from the class.

- If students don't know what an 'elevator pitch' is, explain that it's a short description of an idea that the listener can understand in a short period of time (in other words, the time it takes to take a short elevator ride, or about a minute).

5–10 mins

Work It Out with Business Idioms

2

15–20 mins

- Have students work in pairs.
- Give each pair a copy of **Handout 4.1**.
- Have students read the six tips for making an effective elevator pitch. When they have finished, ask them if they agree that these tips are useful. Ask if there are any additional tips they would add.
- Have students underline the eight idioms they find.
- Elicit answers.
- Ask students to write the idiom that matches its definition at the bottom of the handout.
- Elicit answers.

Extra support
If students have difficulty identifying the idioms in the text, give them a hint by telling them how many idioms are in each tip. (Tip 1 = 2 idioms; Tip 2 = 1 idiom; Tip 3 = 1 idiom; Tip 4 = 1 idiom; Tip 5 = 2 idioms; Tip 6 = 1 idiom)

Answer key Handout 4.1	1 a no-brainer 2 beat around the bush 3 cut to the chase 4 do it with your eyes closed 5 fall on deaf ears 6 go overboard 7 in the market for something 8 put your best foot forward

3

25–30 mins

- Have students work in groups of four.
- Give one student a copy of **Handout 4.2**, one a copy of **Handout 4.3**, one a copy of **Handout 4.4** and one a copy of **Handout 4.5**.
- Explain that they each have an example of an elevator pitch at the top of their handout.
- Students read their elevator pitches silently to themselves. Tell them that they are going to give the pitch as if it's their own. Encourage them to study the text for its key points. They do not need to memorise it exactly.
- Allow them about five minutes to internalise the key points. They may wish to practise their pitch.
- Have Student A stand up and give their elevator pitch to the other three students (Students B–D) in their group. While Student A gives their pitch, the other three students should look at *Feedback form 1* on their handout and tick the boxes whenever the statement is true for the speaker.
- After Student A has given their pitch, Student B then gives their pitch.

Work out 4: Presentations

- The other three students in the group complete *Feedback form 1* on their handout. (Note that *Feedback form 2* will be used in the next section.)
- After all the pitches have been made, ask each group to determine whose pitch was the most effective, and why. Refer them back to the tips in Handout 4.1 and their responses from each Feedback form 1.
- Elicit ideas from the class.

Fast finishers
Have students improve their pitches with their own ideas.

Answer key	Answers will vary
Handouts 4.2–4.5	

4
- Have students remain in their groups of four.
- Tell them that they are now going to prepare their own one-minute elevator pitch.

25–30 mins

- Ask students to prepare ideas to make an elevator pitch to a potential new client. They do not need to write out the pitch – they can take notes on the key points to include.
- Remind students to focus on what their company can offer a new client.
- Tell students that they can use their own name, position and company, or they can invent these. They have just one minute to speak to a new client and make a good impression.
- Refer students back the tips from Handout 4.1 if needed.
- Allow 10 or so minutes for students to prepare and practise their pitches.
- When they are ready, each student should give their elevator pitch to their group.
- While each student is presenting, the other students should complete *Feedback form 2* on their original handout.
- Have students discuss what made each pitch effective.

Fast finishers
Have students revise their pitches based on their group's feedback. Have them give their pitch again.

Work It Out with Business Idioms

> Digital tip
>
> Ask a student in the group to film the presenter using the presenter's phone so they have a record of their pitch. Encourage the presenter to study the video after class to find what they did well and what they could improve upon.

5

15–20 mins

- Before class starts, copy **Teaching tool 4.1** for each group of four. Cut into eight cards and place them face down. (Note that Teaching tool 4.1 contains two sets of identical cards – each team should share a single set of eight cards.)

- Have students work in groups of four. Divide the groups into two pairs: Team 1 and Team 2.

- Player 1 from each team picks a card. They both look at the (same) idiom. They want their teammate (Player 2) to guess the idiom. They can only say *one* word as a clue. They cannot say one of the words in the idiom.

- Player 1 from Team 1 gives a one-word clue. Player 2 from Team 1 gets one guess after hearing the clue. If Player 2 guesses the idiom correctly, Team 1 gets a point. If they guess incorrectly, it's Team 2's turn. Player 1 from Team 2 then gives a one-word clue to their partner.

- If Player 2 from Team 2 guesses correctly, Team 2 gets a point. If no one is able to guess the idiom after receiving three clues each, the card is 'dead' and neither team gets the point.

- Continue until all the idiom cards have been played. Remind students to listen carefully to each clue and try and remember them. The sequence of the clues can be helpful in guessing the idiom.

- Monitor and assist as needed. The team with the most points at the end wins.

> Example: Idiom on card: A no-brainer
>
> Team 1, Player 1: 'body'; Player 2: 'put one's best foot forward' [incorrect answer]
>
> Team 2, Player 1: 'head'; Player 2: 'fall on deaf ears' [incorrect answer]
>
> Team 1, Player 1: 'obvious'; Player 2: 'do something with one's eyes closed' [incorrect answer]
>
> Team 2, Player 1: 'mind'; Player 2: 'a no-brainer' [correct answer]

> Extra challenge
>
> If you have taught more idioms than the ones on the cards, consider reviewing these as well. Create cards with the additional idioms and include them in the pile.

Work out 5

Teamwork

A chain is only as strong as its weakest link. – English proverb

B2+

Resources	Handout 5.1	one copy per pair
	Handout 5.2	one copy per pair
	Handout 5.3	one copy per pair
	Handout 5.4	one copy per student
	Teaching tool 5.1	one copy per group
	Teaching tool 5.2	one copy per group

Target language

All hands on deck – everyone is needed

Go with the flow – to do what everyone else is doing

Have one's ducks in a row – to be well-prepared for what is going to happen

Hold one's tongue – to stop oneself from speaking

Keep one's eye on the prize – to keep one's focus on achieving a goal

Pull out all the stops – to make every possible effort to achieve something

Set one's mind to something – to give something one's complete attention and effort

Stick one's neck out – to expose oneself to some risk

1

- Before class starts, cut up **Teaching tool 5.1** into strips. Tape them in different places on the classroom walls.

- Tell students that you are interested in their ideas about teamwork. Ask them to go and read each of the quotes on the wall.

- After students have read all the quotes, ask them to stand by the quote they most identify with. Encourage students to share their ideas about the quotes with those standing next to them.

- Elicit from individual students why they chose a particular quote. Have them try to put their chosen quote in their own words. Ask if they have personally experienced what the quote says.

- Have students return to their seats.

10–15 mins

> **Digital tip**
>
> As students are choosing the quote they most identify with, have them search online for more information about the author.

Work It Out with Business Idioms

2

15–20 mins

- Have students work in pairs.
- For each pair, give one student a copy of **Handout 5.1** and the other a copy of **Handout 5.2**. Tell students not to look at each other's information.
- Explain that they both have information on four different teamwork styles, but some information is missing. They need to ask their partner questions to complete the missing information.
- Have students work out what questions they need to ask their partner. Have them write out the four questions on their handout. One student asks about The Contributor and the Communicator styles (Handout 5.1), while the other asks about the Collaborator and Challenger styles (Handout 5.2).
- Monitor as each pair completes the questions they need to ask. Provide individual assistance as needed.
- Once the students have written out their questions, have them take turns to ask the questions to their partner to find the missing information. Have them write the answers to their questions in the gaps in the text.
- When they finish asking the questions and writing the answers, tell students to check their answers by sharing their texts with their partner.
- Have students find and underline the eight idioms in the text.

Answer key Handout 5.1	1 What are they good at? (*sharing information with their team members*) 2 What do they care about? (*the details*) 3 How do they ensure that everything goes smoothly? (*by being an active listener and task facilitator*) 4 How do others view the Communicator? (*as a 'people person'*)

Answer key Handout 5.2	1 What do they see their team's mission as? (*the most important thing*) 2 Why do they always keep their eye on their prize? (*because they know it's the ultimate goal*) 3 How are Challengers often described? (*as direct, outspoken, ethical* and *honest*) 4 What are they more willing than others to do? (*to disagree with the team leader*)

3

- Give each pair a copy of **Handout 5.3**. Have the class look at the first question.

15–20 mins

Work out 5: Teamwork

- Ask:

  Are Contributors well-prepared for what is going to happen in their team? (yes)

- Tell students they can refer to Handouts 5.1 and 5.2 to help them find the answers.
- Ask them to write their answers in the *Answers* column of Handout 5.3.
- Have students look at Handout 5.1 or Handout 5.2 again. Ask what words helped them to answer Question 1.
- Elicit the answer (*organised; reliable; always have their ducks in a row*).
- Have students write the words that helped them in the *Which words…?* column of Handout 5.3. If necessary, go over the second question as a class.
- Ask pairs to answer the rest of the questions.
- Elicit answers.

Answer key		Questions	Answers	Which words…?
Handout 5.3	1	Are Contributors well-prepared for what is going to happen in their team?	yes	…organised, reliable; …always have their ducks in a row.
	2	Do Contributors tend to quit when things prove to be challenging?	no	…will pull out all the stops…; …will use any resources available…
	3	Is the ultimate goal for Collaborators to keep their focus on achieving that goal?	yes	…always keep their eye on their prize….
	4	Do Collaborators tend to give something their complete attention and effort?	yes	Once they set their mind to something, there is no stopping them…
	5	Do Collaborators sometimes let others do all the work when a project requires everyone's participation?	no	If what the project requires is all hands on deck, they are happy to do their part.

Work It Out with Business Idioms

	6	Are Collaborators or Communicators more likely to happily go along with what everyone else is doing?	Communicators	They tend to go with the flow.
	7	Do Challengers keep their thoughts to themselves during meetings?	no	They do not tend to hold their tongue…
	8	Are Challengers OK with taking on some risks that others may not?	yes	They will stick their neck out as required.

Extra support

Have students work in small groups instead of pairs.

4
- Have students work in pairs. Give each student a copy of **Handout 5.4**.
15–20 mins
- Ask students to interview each other. Explain that they should take turns to ask each other the questions, stating the four possible choices for each. They should circle their *partner's* responses on their own handout. Monitor the pairs to ensure that students are speaking, and not simply circling their own responses. Remind them that it's good for speaking practice.
- Tell students that, even though it may be difficult to choose just one answer, they should answer with the choice that best describes them.
- When students are finished with their interview, write the following information on the board:

Mostly a answers = a Contributor

Mostly b answers = a Collaborator

Mostly c answers = a Communicator

Mostly d answers = a Challenger

- Ask students if they agree or disagree with the results. Encourage them to provide behavioural examples.

Fast finishers

Ask students to reflect on which teamwork style the survey says they are *least* like, and to discuss whether they agree or disagree.

Work out 5: Teamwork

5
- Have students work in groups of four.
- Tell them that each pair within their groups needs to write a conversation between two speakers of between six and eight lines.
- Explain that the conversation must include two idioms from the lesson. Each conversation should have a context that shows that they have understood the idioms.
- Using **Teaching tool 5.2**, give each pair two (different) idiom cards.
- Give a time limit of 10 minutes for students to think of and write out a conversation. Monitor and assist as needed.
- After both pairs have written their conversations, have them rejoin their group. Have each pair stand up and act out their conversation to the other pair.
- If time allows, ask for a pair or two to act out their conversations for the class.
- Clarify any idioms that have not been fully understood.

15–20 mins

> ### Extra challenge
> Give each pair three idiom cards instead of two. You may wish to do this at the beginning of the activity, or give the third card after they have written their conversations with two idioms.

Work out

Sales and marketing

Don't sell the fish that is still swimming in the ocean. – Turkish proverb

B2+

Resources	Handout 6.1	one copy per pair
	Handout 6.2	one copy per pair
	Handout 6.3	one copy per pair
	Handout 6.4	one copy per group
	Teaching tool 6.1	one copy per group of 8

Target language

Go through the roof – to rise to a very high level

Hit the nail on the head – to describe exactly what's causing a situation or problem

Put (someone) on the spot – to ask someone a question that's difficult to answer

Rack one's brains – to think very hard about something

Step up one's game – to improve one's performance or quality of work

Take (something or somewhere) by storm – to quickly become very popular

Think outside the box – to think in an original or creative way

Up to scratch – good enough or up to the required standard (often used in the negative)

1
- Write the following questions on the board:

    What's the last thing you bought? What influenced your decision to buy it?

    What's an example of a product that has recently sold well in your country?

    Which types of marketing do you think are most effective? least effective?

- Put students in small groups to discuss the questions.
- Elicit ideas from the class.

5–10 mins

2
- Have students work in pairs.
- Give each pair a copy of the cut-up conversation in **Handout 6.1**.

10–15 mins

Work out 6: Sales and marketing

- Ask the class:

  How many people are participating in the meeting? (three)

  What section is the first part of the conversation? (C)

  What's the purpose of the meeting? (to discuss a drop in sales)

- Ask students to underline the idioms they find.

- Have students put the rest of the conversation strips in order. Monitor and provide support as needed.

- Elicit answers by asking a pair to read their ordered conversation. Other pairs should check that they have the same order.

Extra support

If students have difficulty identifying the idioms in the conversation, provide hints by saying one word from each idiom (e.g. *spot, roof, storm, scratch, hit, game, outside, rack*).

Fast finishers

As pairs finish, ask them to think of a possible way to reverse the decline in sales in Asia.

Answer key	1 C	2 I	3 E	4 D	5 H	6 A
Handout 6.1	7 J	8 G	9 B	10 K	11 F	

3
- Give each pair a copy of **Handout 6.2**. Have the class look at the first question. Ask:

  Who first asks Adam a question that's difficult to answer? (Caroline)

15–20 mins

- Tell students they can refer to Handout 6.1 to help them find the answers.

- Ask them to write their answers in the *Answers* column of Handout 6.2.

- Have students look at Handout 6.1 again. Ask which words helped them to answer Question 1.

- Elicit the answer (*I don't mean to put you on the spot*).

- Have students write the words that helped them in the *Which words…?* column of Handout 6.2.

- If necessary, go over the second question as a class.

Work It Out with Business Idioms

- o Ask pairs to answer the rest of the questions.
- o Elicit answers.

Answer key		Questions	Answers	Which words...?
Handout 6.2	1	Who first asks Adam a question that's difficult to answer?	Caroline	...I don't mean to put you on the spot...
	2	Have sales gone up or down in the Americas?	up	...they've gone through the roof.
	3	Has Chico Choco's new chocolate bar quickly become popular in East Asia?	yes	...it's taken the region by storm.
	4	Does Adam think his company's social media ads are good enough?	no	...aren't really up to scratch...
	5	Does Caroline think Adam describes exactly why Chico Choco succeeded?	yes	...you really hit the nail on the head...
	6	Does Caroline think their company needs to improve its performance?	yes	...we clearly need to step up our game...
	7	Does Caroline think they should copy Chico Choco's chocolate bar quickly, or think of their own solution in a more creative way?	think of their own solution in more creative way	...we can come up with something creative if we think outside the box.
	8	Does Caroline suggest that they think very hard or take a break after viewing some videos?	think very hard	Let's view some of their videos and then rack our brains...

4

- o Give each pair a copy of **Handout 6.3**.
- o Ask the pairs to complete the questions with the words in the box. Remind them that two words are extra and are not used.

20–25 mins

Work out 6: Sales and marketing

- o If students cannot remember all the idioms, they can look back at Handout 6.1 for help.
- o Elicit answers.
- o Have pairs join another pair. Ask them to discuss each question. Tell them each student should answer each question.

Fast finishers
Tell students to write additional questions using the idioms. Then, have them discuss the questions.

Answer key Handout 6.3	1 roof 2 rack 3 spot 4 storm 5 scratch 6 nail 7 step 8 box

5
- o Have students work in small groups.
- o Give each group a copy of **Handout 6.4**. Go over the information with the class. Explain any of the marketing strategies they don't know or ask others to do so, or allow students to search online.
- o Explain that each group needs to come up with some marketing ideas for a new product.
- o Tell the groups to think outside the box and to try to come up with some creative ideas. Give a time limit of 20 minutes.
- o Encourage students to use the idioms they've learned in their discussion.
- o Monitor and assist as needed. Encourage the groups to come up with different strategies for each market. They do not need to go into great detail on their plans.
- o After they have finished, ask one or two people from each group to present their ideas to the class. Encourage students to ask questions about the marketing idea.

30–40 mins

Extension activity
Ask the class what they felt were the best ideas they heard. As a class, come up with a single plan. Ask them if they have any ideas for a slogan for the new product.

6
- o Before class starts, copy **Teaching tool 6.1** for every eight students. If you have more than eight students, have pairs share cards. Cut into 16 cards: 8 idioms and 8 definitions. You may wish to copy the idioms and the definitions on different colours of paper.

15–20 mins

- Tell students that they will each receive two cards: an idiom card and a definition card. Be sure that the idiom card and the definition card do **not** match. They will need to find the person who has the definition of their idiom card, and at the same time they will need to find the person who has the idiom that matches their definition card.

- Have students hold the idiom card in their *right* hand, and the definition card in their *left* hand.

- When they find a match, tell students to stand next to that person. As students start making matches, have them form a single, larger circle.

- Before starting the activity, ask the following comprehension questions.

    What is in your right hand? (an idiom card)

    What is in your left hand? (a definition card)

    Does the idiom match the definition? (no)

    What do you do when you find a match? (Stand to the right or left of the person)

    What is the ultimate goal? (to make a single circle)

- Start the activity. Monitor to make sure that students are on task.

- When they finish, check answers by going around the circle, having a student say the idiom and the person next to them say the definition. That student then says their idiom, and the student next to them says the definition, and so on.

Work out 7

Problem-solving

There's more than one way to skin a cat. – English proverb

B2+

Resources	Handout 7.1	one copy per pair
	Handout 7.2	one copy per pair
	Handout 7.3	one copy per pair
	Teaching tool 7.1	one copy per group

Target language

A piece of cake – a very easy task

At this stage of the game – at this point in the process or situation

Bite off more than one can chew – to do more than one is capable of

Cross your fingers – to hope for good luck

More than meets the eye – more than there appears to be at first

Par for the course – normal, not unusual at all

Put (something) into action – to implement a plan or idea

Throw cold water on something – to be negative about someone's plan or idea

---

1

- Have students work in groups of four-to-six. Ask each group to stand in a circle facing each other.

- Tell each student to lift their right hand and then grab the right hand of someone across from them.

- Then, tell them to each lift their left hand and grab the left hand of a different person.

- Check to make sure that everyone is holding the hands of two different people.

- Explain that they have a problem: they must untangle themselves to form a circle without breaking the chain of hands.

- Give a time limit of 10 or so minutes to solve the problem. Explain that if the chain of hands is broken at any point, they must start over again.

- When the activity is completed, write the following questions on the board:

15–20 mins

Work It Out with Business Idioms

Were you successful in solving the problem?

Was it an easy problem to solve? Why or why not?

What process did your group follow as you tried to solve the problem?

- o Put students in small groups to discuss the questions.
- o Elicit ideas from the class.

Extra support
Assign a 'director' who is not part of the circle, but who instructs the group on how to untangle their knot.

Extra challenge
Try the activity again with a larger number of students in each circle.

2

- o Have students work in pairs.
- o Tell them that they are going to read about a five-step method for solving a problem. Give each pair a copy of **Handout 7.1**.
- o Ask them to read the text, and then to work together to determine which sentence goes into each blank. Monitor and assist as needed.
- o Elicit answers from the class.
- o Have students underline the eight idioms they find.
- o Ask them if they followed the five steps when they tried to untangle themselves at the beginning of the lesson.

15–20 mins

Extra support
If students have difficulty identifying the idioms in the text, tell them how many idioms appear in each step (Step 1: 1; Step 2: 2; Step 3: 1; Step 4: 1; Step 5: 3).

Fast finishers
Ask students to discuss whether or not they agree with the five steps. Determine whether they want to omit any information because it's not helpful or needed, or add any information to improve the process of problem-solving.

Answer key Handout 7.1	1 d 2 b 3 e 4 a 5 c

3

o Give each pair a copy of **Handout 7.2**. Have the class look at the first question. Ask:

15–20 mins

When you look at a problem, is there sometimes more to it than what may appear at first? (yes)

o Tell students they can refer to Handout 7.1 to help them find the answers.

o Ask them to write their answers in the *Answers* column of Handout 7.2.

o Have students look at Handout 7.1 again. Ask which words helped them to answer Question 1.

o Elicit the answer (*there may be more than meets the eye*).

o Have students write the words that helped them in the *Which words...?* column of Handout 7.2.

o If necessary, go over the second question as a class.

o Ask pairs to answer the rest of the questions.

o Elicit answers.

Answer key		Questions	Answers	Which words...?
Handout 7.2	1	When you look at a problem, is there sometimes more to it than what may appear at first?	yes	There may be more than meets the eye.
	2	Should you say that an idea is bad during the brainstorming process?	no	Don't throw cold water on any idea. At this stage in the game, don't worry if the ideas are good or bad.
	3	Is it normal to feel overwhelmed by a large number of possible solutions?	yes	...this is par for the course...
	4	Does everyone find it challenging to decide on a solution?	no	This is a piece of cake for some people...
	5	When it's time to take action, is it a good idea to try and do more than you're capable of?	no	Don't bite off more than you can chew...

Work It Out with Business Idioms

	6	Do you implement your plan before or after you get any necessary approvals?	after	...then put your plan into action.
	7	Is there something you can do to show that you hope for good luck?	yes	...cross your fingers...

4
- Have students work in pairs.
- Give each pair a copy of **Handout 7.3**. Ask them to check that the eight underlined idioms are the same as the ones that they underlined in Handout 7.1.
- Ask students to circle the meaning (a or b) of each underlined idiom.
- Elicit answers.
- Ask the class several questions using the idioms. For example:

Are long working hours par for the course at your company?

Has this lesson been a piece of cake so far? Why or why not?

Have you ever bitten off more than you can chew at work or school? In what way?

Has a coworker or boss ever thrown cold water on an idea you've had? What was the idea?

At this stage of the game, is learning and remembering new idioms getting easier?

15–20 mins

Answer key Handout 7.3	1 a 2 a 3 b 4 b 5 a 6 a 7 a 8 b

5
- Before class starts, copy **Teaching tool 7.1** for each group. Cut into six discussion cards.
- Have students work in groups. Give each group a set of cards and ask them to place the cards face down in front of them.
- Tell students they are going to read about six different work problems. Ask them to pick up the cards and discuss each problem one at a time. Encourage them to ask follow-up questions to find out the reasons for each person's opinion.

20–25 mins

Work out 7: Problem-solving

- Tell students to try to reach a consensus on what to do, but assure them that it's fine if there is disagreement among the group members.
- Set a time limit of around 15–20 minutes so that students can monitor and pace their discussion.
- When they have discussed all the questions, elicit ideas from the class.

> Variation
>
> Assign each student a role for the discussion. Possible roles you could assign include:
>
> *The facilitator*: manages the task to ensure that everyone remains focused, as well as make sure that everyone participates in the discussion
>
> *The recorder*: keeps a written record of all the ideas that are discussed and the solution the group ultimately decides on
>
> *The spokesperson*: summarises and presents the group's ideas to the class, using the recorder's notes to guide their report
>
> *The questioner*: pushes back if the group reaches a consensus too quickly, without considering a number of solutions or points of view
>
> *The encourager*: encourages group members to 'dig deep' and continue to think through their approaches and ideas
>
> *The timekeeper*: keeps the group aware of any time limits so as to ensure each discussion is covered adequately

6   *10–15 mins*

- Divide the class into two teams.
- Place two chairs at the front of the room so that they are facing the class. These are the 'hot seats'.
- Invite one student from each team to sit in a hot seat.
- Write an idiom on the board so the class (but not those in the hot seats) can read it.
- Students describe the idiom – to their teammate in the hot seat – by using synonyms, antonyms and definitions. They are not allowed to say any of the words in the idioms.
- The first hot seat student to say the exact idiom wins a point for their team.
- Invite two new students to sit in the hot seats.
- Continue until you have covered all eight of the idioms from the lesson.

Work out **8**

Global branding

'Eighty-nine percent of shoppers stay loyal to brands that share their values.' – *Wantedness*

B2+

Resources	Handout 8.1	one copy per pair
	Handout 8.2	one copy per pair
	Teaching tool 8.1	one copy per group
	Teaching tool 8.2	one copy per group

Target language

At the eleventh hour – at the latest possible moment

Come up smelling like roses – to emerge from a difficult situation successfully

Cut the mustard – to be adequate enough (often used in the negative)

Get into hot water – to get into trouble

Have egg on one's face – to appear foolish

Hit pay dirt (US) – to make a lot of money quickly

Take a nosedive – to drop quickly

The ins and outs – the particular details of a situation

1
- Write the following questions on the board:

    What do you think are the most successful global brands?

    What has made these brands so successful?

    What are some ways in which a company can build its brand globally?

- Put students in small groups to discuss the questions.
- Elicit ideas from the class.

5–10 mins

2
- Have students work in pairs. Give each pair a copy of **Handout 8.1**.
- Have students read the text. Ask whether they know of any other examples similar to those mentioned in the text.
- Have students underline the eight idioms they find.

15–20 mins

Work out 8: Global branding

- o Elicit answers.
- o Ask students to write the idiom that matches its definition at the bottom of the handout.
- o Elicit answers.

Answer key Handout 8.1	1 took a nosedive	2 got into hot water
	3 had egg on its face	4 at the eleventh hour
	5 the ins and outs	6 hit pay dirt
	7 cut the mustard	8 came up smelling like roses

Extra support
If students experience difficulty identifying the idioms in the text, give them a hint by telling them how many idioms are in each tip. (Opening paragraph = 1 idiom; Tip 1 = 1 idiom; Tip 2 = 2 idioms; Tip 3 = 2 idioms; Tip 4 = 2 idioms.)

3

- o Give each pair a copy of **Handout 8.2**. Have the class look at the first question. Ask:

15–20 mins

  Is it more important to have a general understanding of another culture, or the full details? (the full details)

- o Tell students they can refer to Handout 8.1 to help them find the answers.
- o Ask them to write their answers in the *Answers* column of Handout 8.2.
- o Have students look at Handout 8.1 again. Ask which words helped them to answer Question 1.
- o Elicit the answer (*need to learn the ins and outs*).
- o Have students write the words that helped them in the *Which words…?* column of Handout 8.2.
- o If necessary, go over the second question as a class.
- o Ask pairs to answer the rest of the questions.
- o Elicit answers.

Answer key Handout 8.2		Questions	Answers	Which words…?
	1	Is it more important to have a general understanding of another culture, or the full details?	the full details	…need to learn the ins and outs…

	2	Did Walmart expect to struggle in China for a while, or make money quickly?	make money quickly	...expect to hit pay dirt.
	3	When Boston Chicken expanded, was its name a problem?	yes	...no longer cut the mustard.
	4	Was the result of Boston Chicken's name change positive or negative?	positive	...was a smart move ... came up smelling like roses.
	5	Did Dolce and Gabbana get into trouble for its ad in China?	yes	...got into hot water ... The Chinese government criticised the ad...
	6	Did Dolce and Gabbana's sales in China go up because of its ad campaign?	no	...sales took a nosedive.
	7	Did the company Kiri change its name in Iran right away?	no	...at the eleventh hour...
	8	How would Kiri have appeared if it hadn't made the name change?	foolish	The company definitely would have had egg on its face if...

4

- Before class starts, copy **Teaching tool 8.1** for each group. Cut into six discussion cards.

20–25 mins

- Have students work in groups. Give each group a set of cards and ask them to place the cards face down in front of them.

- Tell students that they are going to read about six different global-branding failures. Ask them to take turns to pick up a card and read or summarise it to their group members.

- Ask them to discuss how serious the failure was. Then, ask them to relate it to the text in Handout 8.1. Ask what the company should have done to avoid the failure.

- After they have read and discussed all the cards, ask students to determine which failure was the most serious, and why. Have them rank the failures from 1 (most serious) to 6 (least serious).

Work out 8: Global branding

o Elicit opinions.

> **Extension activity**
>
> Have student think of one international product that has sold well in their country and one that has not. Ask them to explain why one sold well while the other didn't.

5

o Before class starts, copy **Teaching tool 8.2** for each group. Cut each set into eight cards.

10–15 mins

o Have the students work in groups of four. Divide each group into pairs: Team 1 and Team 2.

o Give each group a set of eight cards, placed face down. Tell the groups that each card contains an idiom.

o Player 1 from Team 1 stands up and pick a card. Player 1 has 30 seconds to try to get Player 2 from their team to say the idiom without using words or sounds. They can only use gestures and act out the idiom to try to get their partner to guess.

o If Player 2 can guess the idiom, Team 1 gets the card and one point. They get only two guesses.

o If Player 2 cannot guess correctly, Team 2 can 'steal' the card and point by guessing. They get only one guess.

o Insist on the exact wording of each idiom, except for pronouns. For example, it's OK to say *have egg on your face* or *have egg on his face* instead of *have egg on one's face*. However, do not accept *come up smelling like the rose* for *come up smelling like roses*.

o Player 1 from Team 2 then gets a turn, picking up a card and trying to get Player 2 of their team to guess the idiom. Continue in the same way until they all the idiom cards have been acted out.

o The team with the most points at the end is the winner.

> **Extra support**
>
> Choose an idiom from another lesson to demonstrate the game. Show how to indicate the number of words in the idiom – for example, by holding up a number of fingers to show how many words the idiom contains.

Work out **9**

Customer relations

You can catch more flies with honey than with vinegar.
– English proverb

B2+

Resources	Handout 9.1	one copy per pair
	Handout 9.2	one copy per pair
	Handout 9.3	one copy per pair
	Handout 9.4	one copy per student
	Teaching tool 9.1	As required

Target language

Ahead of the curve – ahead of current thinking or trends

At the end of one's rope (US) – having no strength or patience left

Bang for one's buck (US) – good value for money

Get hold of (someone) – to manage to contact someone

Get the ball rolling – to do something that starts an activity

Get to the bottom of something – to find an explanation for something

No strings attached – having no conditions or expectations in an agreement

To cut a long story short – to explain what happened in a few words

---

1

5–10 mins

- Ask the class what the term 'customer relations' means. Elicit ideas. (*the ways a company engages with its customers to improve the customer experience.*)

- Tell the class that you are going to say several sentences that begin *Stand up if you…*. If their answer is 'yes', they should stand up. If their answer is 'no', they should remain seated.

- Ask the questions one at a time. After each sentence, have the students sit down before you read the next one.

Sentences:

Stand up if you have ever read an online review.

Stand up if you have ever written a negative review.

Stand up if you have ever written a positive review.

Stand up if you have ever written a response to a review.

Work out 9: Customer relations

Stand up if you think a company should ignore negative reviews.

Stand up if you think a company should respond to positive reviews.

Stand up if you think customer-service workers have an easy job.

Stand up if you think the customer is always right.

- o After you say the final sentence, ask students why they feel the customer is or isn't always right.

- o Ask the class if anyone would like to offer their own sentence. Remind them to begin the sentence *Stand up if you…*

2

- o Have students work in pairs.

- o Give each pair a copy of the cut-up conversations in **Handout 9.1**. Explain that they have two phone conversations that are mixed up. They will need to work together to separate the two conversations and put them in order.

15–20 mins

- o Ask the class:

What section is the first part of Conversation 1? (K)

What section is the first part of Conversation 2? (J)

- o Have students put the rest of the two conversation strips in order. Monitor and provide support as needed.

- o Elicit answers by asking a pair to read one of the correctly ordered conversations. Other pairs should check whether they have the same order.

- o Then, ask a different pair to read the other conversation. Other pairs should again check to see that they have the same order.

- o Ask students to underline the idioms they find.

- o Have students summarise orally what each conversation is about.

- o Elicit answers.

Extra support
If students have difficulty identifying the idioms in the two conversations, provide hints by saying one word from the idiom (e.g. *ahead, buck, strings, hold, end, long, bottom, ball*).

Fast finishers
As pairs finish, ask them to role play the two conversations.

Work It Out with Business Idioms

Answer key	Conversation 1: K C I G A M E
Handout 9.1	Conversation 2: J D N H B L F

3
- Have students work in pairs.
- Give each pair a copy of **Handout 9.2**.
- Ask students to read through the questions and then choose the correct answer choice (a or b) for each question.
- Elicit answers.
- Have each pair join another pair to make a group.
- Tell groups to discuss each question. Encourage them to ask follow-up questions to get more information.

20–25 mins

Extension activity
Have one or two students share any interesting answers they heard in their discussions.

Answer key								
Handout 9.2	1 b	2 a	3 a	4 b	5 a	6 a	7 b	8 a

4
- Have students work in pairs.
- Give each pair a copy of **Handout 9.3**.
- Ask pairs to read through the reviews and replace the crossed-out words with idioms from the lesson.
- Elicit answers.
- Tell students to imagine that these are reviews about their own company, or a company they know. Have each student work individually to write responses to the three reviewers.
- Have students share their responses with their partners.
- Ask one or two students to read their responses to the class.

20–25 mins

Digital tip
If the students' companies have an online presence, have them search for reviews. Ask whether the reviews are generally positive or negative, and what they are mainly about. Ask students whether they think the reviews are fair.

Work out 9: Customer relations

Answer key Handout 9.3	1 ahead of the curve	2 bang for your buck
	3 no strings attached	4 get to the bottom of
	5 get hold of	6 to cut a long story short

5

20–25 mins

- Have students work alone.
- Give each student a copy of **Handout 9.4**.
- Tell the class that the table lists six ways to build customer loyalty. Tell students to read through the list, considering each one, and then tick the **five** ways that they feel are the most important in the 'You' column. Monitor to make sure students are marking their ideas correctly in the correct column.
- After they have marked their choices, have each student join a partner. Ask them to compare their opinions and support these with reasons. Then, tell pairs to agree on and tick the **four** ways that they feel are most important in the 'Pair' column. Explain that they should try to persuade their partner to agree with them, but, ultimately, they may have to compromise to come to an agreement. Continue to monitor. You may want to provide a time limit of about five minutes.
- When most have agreed on the top four, have each pair then join another pair to form a group. Ask groups to compare and discuss their opinions. Tell them to agree on and tick the **three** ways that the group believes are most important in the 'Group' column. You may again want to provide a time limit of about five or more minutes.
- When the groups have come to an agreement, elicit ideas from the class. Lead a short class discussion.

Fast finishers

Have students add to the table one more way to build customer loyalty.

6

10–15 mins

- Divide the class into two or three teams.
- Explain that you are going to read out three clues, one at a time (using **Teaching tool 9.1**). The clues describe an idiom from the lesson.
- Each team can try and guess the idiom only one time. Insist that you will accept only one guess, so they should discuss as needed to be sure that they are happy with the guess.
- The first team to guess the idiom correctly gets a point. If a team makes a wrong guess, or makes an important error, they are out of the round and must wait until the next idiom.

- o Give the first clue. If no one chooses to guess, proceed to the second clue.
- o Give the second clue. If no one chooses to guess, proceed to the third and final clue.
- o Give the third cue.
- o Use your best judgement when deciding to accept or not accept an answer. For example, accept *bang for your buck* for *bang for one's buck*, but do not accept *to get a ball rolling* for *get the ball rolling*.

Teaching tool 9.1
1 This idiom contains three words. 2 The first word is the opposite of 'yes'. 3 It means 'having no conditions or expectations in an agreement'. **No strings attached**
1 You might hear this idiom at the beginning of a meeting. 2 One word is something you see in a soccer match. 3 It means 'to do something that starts an activity'. **Get the ball rolling**
1 You want a product that offers this. 2 This idiom contains four words. 3 The first and the last words begin with the letter 'B'. **Bang for one's buck**
1 This idiom can be used to start a sentence. 2 It contains two words that are opposites of each other. 3 You use this to explain what happened in just a few words. **To cut a long story short**
1 The idiom begins with a short preposition. 2 The last word rhymes with the word 'nope'. 3 You say this when you have no strength or patience left. **At the end of one's rope**
1 This idiom is related to communication. 2 You might feel frustrated if you cannot do this. 3 You can do this by text or by phone. **Get hold of someone**
1 You would probably be relieved if you do this. 2 A detective or police officer would want to do this. 3 One word in the idiom is the opposite of the word 'top'. **Get to the bottom of something**
1 Many companies would like to be described in this way. 2 The second word is 'of'. 3 The last word rhymes with the word 'serve'. **Ahead of the curve**

Work out 9: Customer relations

Digital tip
You may wish to use a presentation tool to reveal the clues (and later the idiom) one at a time.

Extra challenge
If you have taught more idioms, consider reviewing these as well. Create your own clues with the additional idioms.

Work out 10

Corporate Social Responsibility (CSR)

'The business of business should not be about money, It should be about responsibility.' – Anita Roddick

B2+

Resources	Handout 10.1	one copy per student
	Handout 10.2	one copy per pair
	Handout 10.3	one copy per pair
	Handout 10.4	one copy per pair
	Handout 10.5	one copy per pair
	Teaching tool 10.1	one copy per class
	Teaching tool 10.2	one copy per group

Target language

A force to be reckoned with – a person or thing that is strong and powerful

A win-win situation – a situation that is good for everyone involved

Between a rock and a hard place – in a situation with two equally bad alternatives

Cost (someone) an arm and a leg – to be very expensive

From the get-go (US) – from the very beginning

Make a fast buck (US) – to earn money quickly and easily

Strapped for cash – having little or no money at the moment

Stretch the truth – to say something that's not exactly true (to make a situation seem better)

1
- Write the following questions on the board:

    How important is it for corporations to practise social responsibility?

    In which areas can corporations develop a strategy for being more socially responsible?

    Are there products you won't buy for ethical reasons? If so, what are they?

- Put students in small groups to discuss the questions.
- Elicit ideas from the class.

5–10 mins

Work out 10: Corporate Social Responsibility (CSR)

2

20–25 mins

- Before class starts, cut up **Teaching tool 10.1** into the six parts. Tape each part in a different place on the walls of the classroom.
- Have students work alone. Explain that they are going to read about three advantages of Corporate Social Responsibility, as well as three disadvantages.
- Give each student a copy of **Handout 10.1**.
- Tell students to walk to and read the texts on the walls, one by one. As they read, ask them to take notes on each text's key ideas and to write them under the correct column (*Advantages* and *Disadvantages*) in the table.
- When students have finished, they should take their seats and compare their notes with a partner's.
- Elicit answers from the class.
- Ask students whether they can think of any other advantages or disadvantages.

Answer key	Advantages	Disadvantages
Handout 10.1 *Possible answers*	Image improvement - corporations improve reputation - consumers feel good - builds trust	Increased production costs - can be expensive - can lead to price increases for the consumer - challenging for small businesses
	Employee satisfaction - easier to find and keep employees - people want to work for corporations that care	Profits in conflict - duty to maximise profits - some managers could lose their jobs if they focus too much on social responsibility
	Customer loyalty - millennials like corporations with pro-social messages - more likely to be loyal to the brand	'Greenwashing' - term that means only appearing to be socially responsible - not all consumers see this as not being truthful

3

15–20 mins

- Have students work in pairs.
- Give each pair a copy of **Handout 10.2**.
- Ask students to read the whole text again.
- Tell students to underline the eight idioms in the text.

Work It Out with Business Idioms

- Elicit answers.
- Ask students to write the idioms at the bottom of the handout to complete the definitions. Elicit answers.

Answer key Handout 10.2	1 from the get-go; 2 cost (someone) an arm and a leg; 3 make a fast buck; 4 strapped for cash; 5 a win-win situation; 6 a force to be reckoned with; 7 between a rock and a hard place; 8 stretch the truth

Extra support
If students have difficulty identifying the idioms in the text, provide hints by saying one word from the idiom (e.g. *situation, from, force, fast, cost, cash, between, truth*).

4

- Give each pair a copy of **Handout 10.3**. Have the class look at the first question. Ask:

  15–20 mins

  Who wins when a corporation improves its reputation as a result of its approach to corporate social responsibility? (corporations and consumers)

- Tell students to refer to Handout 10.2 to help them find the answers.
- Ask students to write their answers in the *Answers* column of Handout 10.3.
- Have students look at Handout 10.2 again. Ask what words helped them answer the question.
- Elicit the answer (*a win-win situation*).
- Have students write the words that helped them in the *Which words …?* column of Handout 10.3. If necessary, go over the second question as a class.
- Ask pairs to answer the rest of the questions.
- Elicit answers.

Answer key		Questions	Answers	Which words…?
Handout 10.3	1	Who wins when a corporation improves its reputation as a result of its approach to corporate social responsibility?	corporation and consumers	…a win-win situation.

Work out 10: Corporate Social Responsibility (CSR)

	2	Do socially responsible corporations find it easier to keep employees if they start their CSR efforts early?	yes	...from the get-go...
	3	Do millennials have much power these days?	yes	...a force to be reckoned with...
	4	Do millennials often prefer to do business with corporations that earn money quickly and easily?	no	...just out to make a fast buck.
	5	Does it cost much money for a corporation to be socially responsible?	yes	...cost a corporation an arm and a leg...
	6	What don't small businesses often have enough of?	money / cash	...can be strapped for cash...
	7	Do management teams that only focus on increasing profits for shareholders find themselves in a good position?	no	...can put them between a rock and a hard place.
	8	Are corporations that engage in 'greenwashing' being honest?	no	...others see them as stretching the truth.

5
- Have student work in pairs.
- For each pair, give one student a copy of **Handout 10.4** and the other a copy of **Handout 10.5**. Tell students not to look at each other's information.
- Explain that they both have information on what eight companies have done to become more socially responsible, but some information is missing. They will need to ask their partner questions to complete the missing information.
- Have students work out what questions they will need to ask their partner. The questions begin with the question word provided after

25–30 mins

Work It Out with Business Idioms

- each gap. Tell them to look at the sentence and keep the question in the same grammar tense.
- o Monitor while each pair takes turns to ask questions to find the missing information. Provide individual assistance as needed.
- o Have students write the answers to their questions in the gaps.
- o When they have finished asking the questions and writing the answers, tell students to check their answers by sharing their texts with their partner.
- o Have them find and underline the eight idioms in each text.
- o When the activity is completed, write the following questions on the board:

What has each company done to be more socially responsible?

Which three initiatives are you most impressed by? Why?

What other companies practise being socially responsible? How?

- o Put students in small groups to discuss the questions.
- o Elicit ideas from the class.

Answer key Handouts 10.4 and 10.5	1 What has Lego also invested heavily in? (*alternative energy sources*)
	2 How much of its net profits does TOMS give to charities that support physical and mental health? (*a third*)
	3 How has Johnson & Johnson reduced its carbon footprint? (*by investing in cleaner energy*)
	4 Who does Starbucks hire? (*veterans, refugees and people who are looking to start their careers*)
	5 What is Google also known for? (*standing up against discrimination*)
	6 How many weeks of paid time off does Netflix offer to new parents? (*52*)
	7 For how long has Patagonia insisted that its employees receive a wage that is above the minimum wage? (*from the get-go*)
	8 What does the drug company Pfizer focus on? (*corporate citizenship*)

6

- o Before class starts, copy **Teaching tool 10.2** for each group. Cut into eight discussion cards.
- o Have students work in small groups. Give each group a set of cards and ask them to place the cards face down in front of them.

10–15 mins

Work out 10: Corporate Social Responsibility (CSR)

- Ask students to take turns to pick up a card, reading the question aloud before answering it. Others in the group should ask follow-up questions to get more information.
- The other students then answer the question on the card.
- The next student then picks up a card. Continue as before until all the questions have been discussed.
- Lead a short class discussion. Elicit any answers that the students found particularly interesting.

Work out 11

Leadership

A gentle hand may lead even an elephant by a hair. – Iranian proverb

B2+

Resources		
	Handout 11.1	one copy per pair
	Handout 11.2	one copy per pair
	Handout 11.3	one copy per pair
	Handout 11.4	one copy per student
	Teaching tool 11.1	one copy for the class
	Teaching tool 11.2	one copy per group

Target language

Bend over backwards – to work extra hard to do something

Bring (something) to the table – to contribute something to a group effort

Call the shots – to tell others what to do

Down the line – at a later date

Go the extra mile – to do more than what is required

On the same page – in agreement on how things should be done

Set the bar high – to establish a high standard of quality

Toe the line – to follow the rules without causing trouble

1
- Write the following questions on the board:

    Who are some important leaders? What fields are they in?

    What qualities make a good leader?

    Do you think you're a good leader? Why or why not?

- Put students in small groups to discuss the questions.

- Elicit ideas from the class.

5–10 mins

2
- Before class starts, cut up **Teaching tool 11.1** into six strips. Tape them in different places around the classroom.

- Have students work in pairs. Give each pair a copy of **Handout 11.1**.

20–25 mins

Work out 11: Leadership

- Tell students that one of them is the 'runner' and the other is the 'writer'.

- Explain that each runner runs to any strip, memorises the letter and sentences, and then returns to dictate it to their partner. If a runner forgets something, they can go back and look again.

- The writer writes the information in the first column next to the appropriate letter (the second column will be used in the next section). Explain that the focus of this work out is on accuracy. Insist on correct spelling, punctuation and capitalisation.

- After three of the sentences are dictated, the students change roles.

- The first pair to finish raises their hands. Check their sentences. Circle the **letter** (A–F) if there are errors, but do not say what the errors are.

- Students continue until they think all sentences are correct. Check each time.

- The first pair to correctly dictate all the sentences without errors is the winner. Stop the activity when most pairs have correct sentences.

- Go over answers with the class. Ask the winning pair to slowly read their correct sentences.

> **Fast finishers**
>
> As each pair finishes, ask them to help others around them by checking sentences against their own. Remind them to circle the letters of the sentences with errors.

3

- Write the following six leadership styles on the board:

  Commanding   Pace-setting   Affiliative
  Democratic   Visionary   Coaching

20–25 mins

- Have students work in pairs to discuss which leadership style they think goes with each description. Ask them to write their guesses in the second column of Handout 11.1.

- Elicit answers from the class.

- Give each pair a copy of **Handout 11.2**. Tell the class to look at the first question. Ask:

  Do Visionary leaders want people to do just enough, or more than is necessary? (Answer: more than is necessary.)

- Encourage students to refer to Handout 11.1 to help them find the answers.

Work It Out with Business Idioms

- o Ask them to write their answers in the *Answers* column of Handout 11.2.
- o Have students look at Handout 11.1 again. Ask what words helped them answer the question.
- o Elicit answer (*go the extra mile*).
- o Have students write the words that helped them in the *Which words…?* column of Handout 11.2.
- o If necessary, go over the second question as a class.
- o Ask pairs to answer the rest of the questions.
- o Elicit answers.

Answer key Handout 11.1	A Visionary B Affiliative C Coaching D Democratic E Pace-setting F Commanding

Answer key		Questions	Answers	Which words…?
Handout 11.2	1	Do Visionary leaders want people to do just enough, or more than is necessary?	more than is necessary	…go the extra mile…
	2	Do Visionary leaders expect people to be in agreement on how things should be done?	yes	…so that everyone is on the same page.
	3	Do Affiliative leaders work extra hard to keep people happy?	yes	…bend over backwards trying to keep everyone happy.
	4	Are Coaching leaders more interested in people's past or future development?	future	…help them to improve those skills down the line.
	5	Are Democratic leaders interested in what other people can contribute?	yes	…are interested in what others can bring to the table.
	6	What level of quality do Pace-setting leaders expect from others?	high	…setting the bar high.

Work out 11: Leadership

	7	Do Commanding leaders let others make important decisions?	no	...top-down decision-making; ...call the shots...
	8	Do Commanding leaders want others to follow the rules they set, or break them?	follow	...expect others to toe the line...

Extra support
Have students work in small groups instead of pairs.

4
- Have students work in pairs.
- Ask them to find and underline the eight idioms they have written in Handout 11.1.
- Give each pair a copy of **Handout 11.3**.
- Ask students to check that the eight underlined idioms in Handout 11.3 are the same idioms that they underlined in Handout 11.1.
- Have pairs circle the meaning (a or b) of each underlined idiom.
- Elicit answers.

15–20 mins

Answer key Handout 11.3	1 a 2 b 3 b 4 b 5 a 6 a 7 b 8 b

Digital tip
Have students search in the 'News' section of a search engine to find real-world examples of the idioms. Remind them to put quotation marks around the idiom when they search.

5
- Have students work in groups of four.
- Give each student a copy of **Handout 11.4**.
- Ask students to discuss each question as a group. Tell them that they do not need to agree on the answers, only to give their own opinion.
- Tell students to ask each other *Why?* to get more information for each response. Encourage them to use idioms in their responses.
- Have students write each other's responses (a–f) in the appropriate column and add any additional notes.

15–20 mins

Work It Out with Business Idioms

- o Tell them to mark their own answers in the last column.

- o When students have finished their discussion, write the following information on the board:

  Mostly a answers = a Democratic leader
  Mostly b answers = a Pace-setting leader
  Mostly c answers = a Commanding leader
  Mostly d answers = a Visionary leader
  Mostly e answers = an Affiliative leader
  Mostly f answers = a Coaching leader

- o Ask students whether they agree or disagree with the quiz results. Mention that a person can have more than one leadership style, depending on the situation.

> Extra support
>
> If students do not know all of the people listed in Question 4, allow them to search for them online.

> Extension activity
>
> Have groups list another leader (alive or dead) for each style. Elicit ideas. Ask the class whether they agree with each group's ideas.

6

15–20 mins

- o Before class starts, copy **Teaching tool 11.2** for each group. Cut into 16 cards.

- o Have students work in groups. Give each group a set of 16 cards.

- o Tell groups to mix all the cards together and spread them face down, in rows, in the centre of a table.

- o The first student chooses a card and turns it over. They then try to find its match (idiom + definition) by turning over another card. The student leaves the two cards face up where they are so all the students can see them.

- o If the cards match, the student keeps both cards. If they don't match, the student turns the cards back over, face down, keeping them in the original place. If they are unsure if there is a match, they can ask you.

- o The next student takes a turn. The group continue to play until all the cards are gone.

- o The student with the most pairs at the end is the winner.

o   If there is time, have students play again.

> **Extra challenge**
>
> Tell students to make a sentence with the idiom after they have found a matching pair. If the sentence does not make sense or shows that the student does not understand the meaning of the idiom, the student loses a turn and must put the cards back in their place.

Work out 12

Job interviews

Choose a job you love, and you will never have to work a day in your life. – Confucius

B2+

> **Resources**
> Handout 12.1   one copy per pair
> Handout 12.2   one copy per pair
> Handout 12.3   one copy per pair
> Handout 12.4   one copy per pair
> Teaching tool 12.1   one copy per group

Target language

In the driver's seat – in control of a situation

Err on the side of caution – to be especially careful rather than take a risk

Go through (something) with a fine-toothed comb – to examine something very closely

Have time to kill – to have a period of time with nothing to do

Keep one's cool – to remain calm and not become upset or angry

Leave no stone unturned – to do everything one can to achieve a goal

Talk someone's ear off – to talk to someone nonstop for a long time

Up in the air – undecided or unresolved

---

1   10–15 mins

- Tell students that you are going to read some possible job interview questions one at a time.

- Tell them to stand up and move to the right side of the room if they think it's an appropriate question to be asked in a job interview. Tell them to stand up and move to the left side of the room if they think it's an inappropriate interview question.

- Read one question. After everyone has moved to the right or left side of the room, elicit several reasons for their choices. Then, read another question.

- After you have asked several questions, ask one or two students to offer their own questions. As before, ask students to move to one side of the room to indicate the appropriateness of each question. Continue as time and interest allows.

- When you are finished, ask students to return to their seats.

Work out 12: Job interviews

Possible questions:

Why do you want this job?

What are your salary expectations?

Why did you leave your last job?

Are you married?

What's your greatest weakness?

Are you willing to work on weekends as needed?

Are you planning to have kids?

In what year did you graduate from college?

If you could be any animal, what would you choose and why?

2
- Have students work in pairs.
- Give each pair a copy of **Handout 12.1**.
- Have students read through the list of interview Do's and Don't's.
- Ask pairs to complete the information with the words in the box. Remind them that four words are extra and are not used.
- If students are finding the task challenging, give them a hint by saying which six possible words go under the Do's (*air, book, caution, hand, stone, time*) and which six possible words go under the Don'ts (*ear, comb, cool, chair, man, seat*).
- Elicit answers.
- Ask students whether they agree with all the Do's and Don't's.
- Elicit opinions.
- Tell pairs to add one more Do and one more Don't to the list.
- Elicit ideas.

15–20 mins

Answer key Handout 12.1	1 stone 2 caution 3 time 4 air 5 comb 6 seat 7 ear 8 cool

Fast finishers

Ask students to share examples of times when they followed or didn't follow the Do's and Don't's during an interview.

Work It Out with Business Idioms

3

15–20 mins

- Give each pair a copy of **Handout 12.2**. Have the class look at the first question. Ask:

  Before an interview, should you do everything you can to find out about the company? (yes)

- Tell students they can refer to Handout 12.1 to help them find the answers.

- Ask them to write their answers in the *Answers* column of Handout 12.2.

- Have students look at Handout 12.1 again. Ask which words helped them to answer Question 1.

- Elicit the answer (*yes*).

- Have students write the words that helped them in the *Which words…?* column of Handout 12.2.

- If necessary, go over the second question as a class.

- Ask pairs to answer the rest of the questions.

- Elicit answers.

Answer key		Questions	Answers	Which words…?
Handout 12.2	1	Before an interview, should you do everything you can to find out about the company?	yes	Leave no stone unturned.
	2	Should you take a risk when you dress for an interview?	no	Err on the side of caution…
	3	What should you do ten minutes before your interview is scheduled to begin?	relax	If you have time to kill beforehand, use it to relax.
	4	Is it good to leave things unresolved regarding the next steps in the interview process?	no	Don't leave the next steps up in the air.
	5	Is it necessary to examine your CV very closely before you send it in?	yes	Go through it with a fine-toothed comb before sending it in.

Work out 12: Job interviews

	6	Who should be in control of the interview – you or the interviewer?	the interviewer	Let the interviewer be in the driver's seat.
	7	During the interview, should you keep talking and talking to the interviewer?	no	Don't talk the interviewer's ear off.
	8	Is it better to be calm, animated or evasive when the interviewer asks you a difficult question?	calm	Keep your cool, even when asked difficult or uncomfortable questions.

4
- Before class starts, equally distribute **Handout 12.3** and **Handout 12.4** to pairs of students.

30–40 mins

- Tell each pair of students that they are going to practise interviewing for a job.

- Tell them to choose whether they wish to be Student A or Student B. Student A will first interview Student B. Then, Student B will interview Student A. Clarify, if necessary, that they will both act as interviewer and interviewee as part of the activity.

- Read the information about the two positions to the class. Explain that the Student As will interview the Student Bs for the position of Social Media Manager, and then the Student Bs will interview the Student As for the position of Flight Attendant.

- Tell each student to think of **five** questions to ask during their interview and to write the questions in the table. Allow a few minutes for this. Monitor and provide guidance, encouraging interesting questions.

- When everyone has written their questions, have students stand up and form two circles. The Student As are outside facing in and the Student Bs are inside facing out. Ask them to stand so that they are face-to-face with their partners.

- Explain that, when you clap your hands, all of the Student As should begin interviewing their partners, asking their five questions. The Student Bs will respond, using idioms from the lesson or other idioms they know if possible. The Student As should not write down the reponses to their questions. Rather, they should maintain eye contact with their interviewees as if they are conducting real interviews. Tell them that you will clap your hands after exactly three minutes.

Work It Out with Business Idioms

- o At this point, all the Student As should quickly give Student Bs a rating of 1, 2 or 3, based on their responses, and then move one place to their left so that they are now facing a new Student B. The Student Bs should not move. The Student As then ask their five questions to the new interviewees.

- o Again, after three minutes, clap your hands. The Student As give their rating and move again to their left. Continue until each Student A has interviewed four candidates.

- o Next, have students switch roles as interviewer and interviewee. Continue as before until the Student Bs have interviewed four candidates.

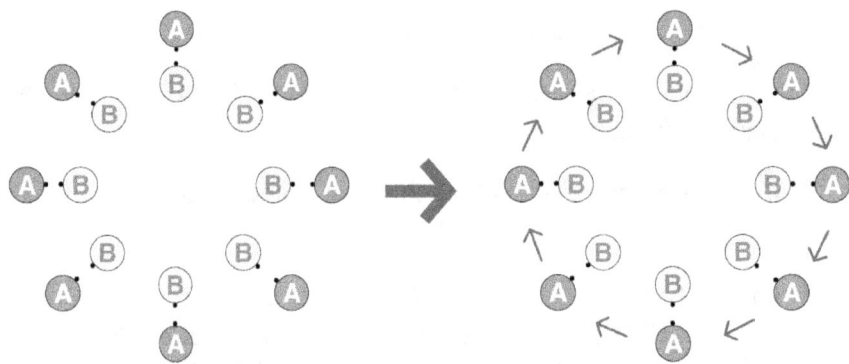

- o Have students return to their seats. Ask them to reflect on who they think is the best candidate for the job, and why.

- o As a class, elicit which interviewer responses were most impressive. Then, ask which interview questions were found to be especially challenging to answer.

> **Variation**
>
> If it's difficult for form a circle in the classroom, have students form two lines instead. When you clap, each Student A moves to the left. The Student A at the far left of the line runs to the far right on the line.

5

- o Before class starts, copy **Teaching tool 12.1** for each group. Cut into eight cards.

10–15 mins

- o Have students work in groups of four.

- o Divide each group into two pairs: Team 1 and Team 2. Put the cards face down on the table between them.

- o Explain that one player from Team 1 will take a card. Player 1 must try to get Player 2 to say the idiom, but Player 1 cannot say the other words on the card to describe it, or repeat any of the words in the idiom itself. If they do, Team 2 gets the card. If Player 1 successfully gets Player 2 to say the idiom, Team 1 keeps the card. Gestures are not allowed.

- Tell students that each player only gets to make two guesses.

- While Player 1 from Team 1 is trying to get Player 2 to say the idiom, students from Team 2 look at the card to make sure that Player 1 doesn't accidentally say one of the words. If they do, Team 2 gets the card. They will also act as timekeeper. Set a time limit of 30 seconds.

- If players are unable to describe and say the idiom, the card is 'dead' and no one gets a point.

- Continue to play with a Player 1 from Team 2 picking up a card and trying to get their Player 2 to say the idiom.

- The team with the most cards/points at the end wins.

> **Extension activity**
> Have groups prepare their own cards, reviewing other idioms they have learned. Ask them to swap their cards with another group and continue to play the game.

Teaching tools

Work It Out with Business Idioms　　　　　　　　　　　　　　　　Teaching tool 1.1

Beat someone to the punch	Get down to business
Get someone up to speed	Have a lot on one's plate
Have money to burn	Not going to fly
Up and running	Work around the clock

to achieve something before someone else does	to start working
to get someone all the information they need	to have many things to do
to have more money than one needs	not going to work well
operating normally	to work all day and all night (to get the job done)

What are soft skills?

A We cannot measure every business skill. We can measure things like the ability to speak a foreign language or use a certain software programme. These are 'hard skills.' As a rule of thumb, include these in your CV, but possessing such skills is only half the battle. Other types of skills are gained through personal relationships and learning the ropes from on-the-job experience. These are 'soft skills' (or 'people skills') and include things like how well we motivate others, or how well we work in a team.

How do I identify my soft skills?

B Ask yourself, 'Has anyone ever praised me for something that involved using a soft skill, such as using my time effectively or stepping up to the plate when needed?' If so, you probably have that skill. Another way is to think about your recent successes at work. You probably used hard skills, but it was a soft skill that pushed you over the finish line. When you identify that skill, you can start to understand how you are using these skills effectively.

Why are soft skills important?

C Soft skills are important tools when building trust and working as part of a team. The bottom line is that soft skills can make the difference between success and failure. Most employers look for hard *and* soft business skills, so it's worth developing both. In a nutshell, a person with both types of skills may tick all the boxes for an employer. Soft skills are also transferable. This means you can take these talents to different jobs and industries.

Work It Out with Business Idioms — Teaching tool 2.2

A rule of thumb	Half the battle
In a nutshell	Learn the ropes
Push someone over the finish line	Step up to the plate
The bottom line	Tick all the boxes

A rule of thumb	Half the battle
In a nutshell	Learn the ropes
Push someone over the finish line	Step up to the plate
The bottom line	Tick all the boxes

Passive Communicators are agreeable, pleasant and well-liked by others. They usually say 'yes' when they are asked to give someone a hand. However, they hardly ever stand up for themselves and often get the short end of the stick. Some people take advantage of them. Passive Communicators sometimes struggle to express negative emotions, so they can get frustrated easily. This can lead to stress and even illness. In short, they tend to focus on others rather than themselves.

Aggressive Communicators take a 'must win' approach. They are direct with other people, and many people appreciate this approach. Aggressive Communicators are honest. They like to 'tell it like it is' and put their cards on the table for all to see and hear. Others may find it hard to get a word in edgeways. One issue is that they are sometimes too focused on their own needs, and not the needs of others. Being aggressive can be useful in the short-term, but being too aggressive too often is harmful to their relationships.

Passive-aggressive Communicators often become frustrated when others don't listen to them. When they speak to others, what they say may go in one ear and out the other. When others do listen, they sometimes say that their input is not valuable. Passive-aggressive Communicators use jokes and humour to get their point across, but take no responsibility for such behaviour. They just say, for example 'I was kidding'. They think others cannot take a joke, or are too sensitive. They may also deny that a problem even exists.

Assertive Communicators are the most balanced of all the communication styles. They look out for themselves, but also show interest in others. They are quick to meet people halfway. Assertive Communicators stand up for their rights, as well as the rights of others. They are happy to help others at the drop of a hat. They are calm, respectful, and well-liked. They are more likely than most to be able to handle challenging situations and people, with little stress. They are also good at building trust and developing personal relationships.

A no-brainer	Beat around the bush
Cut to the chase	Do something with one's eyes closed
Fall on deaf ears	Go overboard
In the market for something	Put one's best foot forward

A no-brainer	Beat around the bush
Cut to the chase	Do something with one's eyes closed
Fall on deaf ears	Go overboard
In the market for something	Put one's best foot forward

'Talent wins games, but teamwork and intelligence win championships.'

– Basketball star Michael Jordan

'Alone we can do so little; together we can do so much.'

– Author and activist Helen Keller

'If you take out the team in teamwork, it's just work. Now who wants that?'

– Novelist Matthew Woodring Stover

'Coming together is a beginning, staying together is progress, and working together is success.'

– Industrialist Henry Ford

It's better to walk alone than with a crowd going in the wrong direction.'

– Playwright Diane Grant

'Individually, we are one drop. Together, we are an ocean.'

– Author Ryūnosuke Satoro

'If you want to go fast, go alone. If you want to go far, go together.'

– African proverb

Work It Out with Business Idioms   Teaching tool 5.2

All hands on deck	Go with the flow
Have one's ducks in a row	Hold one's tongue
Keep one's eye on the prize	Pull out all the stops
Set one's mind to something	Stick one's neck out

All hands on deck	Go with the flow
Have one's ducks in a row	Hold one's tongue
Keep one's eye on the prize	Pull out all the stops
Set one's mind to something	Stick one's neck out

Go through the roof	Hit the nail on the head
Put someone on the spot	Rack one's brains
Step up one's game	Take (something or somewhere) by storm
Think outside the box	Up to scratch

to rise to a very high level	to describe exactly what's causing a situation or problem
to ask someone a question that's difficult to answer	to think very hard about something
to improve one's performance or quality of work	to quickly become very popular
to think in an original or creative way	good enough or up to the required standard

Michael is your new department manager. His expectations of your team are different to those of your previous manager. He does not tell you his expectations until after your team has not met them. This may be par for the course, but how can you learn earlier what Michael's expectations are?	Bernadette in HR is responsible for giving bonuses to employees with perfect attendance during the month. You missed one day due to a death in the family. The rules are clear, but you feel the policy is unfair. How do you get Bernadette to see things your way?
You have just started working for a software start-up. You have a great idea for a new app and share it with your coworker Tomas. He throws cold water on your idea. The next day Tomas presents your idea to your boss as his own idea. The boss loves it and promotes Tomas. What do you do?	Everyone on your sales team works hard to put the new marketing plan into action, except for Jackie. She often conducts personal business during company time and sometimes leaves work early. Your team is still the best, but you feel Jackie is not doing enough. Is there anything you can do?
Your company is planning to expand into Central America and is offering employees free Spanish lessons each morning before work. Brian, your boss, is pressuring you to sign up for the classes, but you need the time before work to get your two children ready for school. What should you do?	You feel may have bitten off more than you can chew at work and now need someone to help you out. You ask your supervisor, Gina, for advice. She asks you what *you* think should be done. You are disappointed in her because you hoped she would lighten your workload. What do you do now?

American Motors once named its new mid-size car *The Matador*. The name was meant to represent strength and courage. The car didn't sell well in Puerto Rico because, in Spanish, *matador* means 'killer'.	The company Gerber got into hot water when it began selling baby food in Africa. The ad showed a cute baby on the label. In many African countries, companies show what is inside the jar on the label for those who are unable to read.
HSBC Bank was left with egg on its face after spending millions of pounds on its 'Assume Nothing' campaign. That's because, in many countries, the slogan was translated as 'Do Nothing'.	Nike once had to recall thousands of its shoes because of an image on its product, a new line of shoes. The image on the back of the shoes was meant to look like fire. However, it resembled the Arabic word for 'Allah'.
Proctor & Gamble makes nappies for babies. When it started selling them in Japan, included in its packaging was an image of a stork (a type of bird) delivering a baby. This works in the UK and US, where it's part of the countries' folklore. Japanese consumers, however, were confused by the image.	The Swedish company Electrolux got a quick lesson in American slang when it tried to sell its latest vacuum cleaner in the US. It used the slogan 'Nothing sucks like an Electrolux'. It should come as no surprise why sales never took off.

Work It Out with Business Idioms   Teaching tool 8.2

At the eleventh hour	Come up smelling like roses
Cut the mustard	Get into hot water
Have egg on one's face	Hit pay dirt
Take a nosedive	The ins and outs

At the eleventh hour	Come up smelling like roses
Cut the mustard	Get into hot water
Have egg on one's face	Hit pay dirt
Take a nosedive	The ins and outs

At the eleventh hour	Come up smelling like roses
Cut the mustard	Get into hot water
Have egg on one's face	Hit pay dirt
Take a nosedive	The ins and outs

Employee satisfaction

The way a corporation treats its community says a lot about how it treats its employees. Corporations with a strong commitment to social responsibility from the get-go find it easier to find and retain employees. People want to work for companies that care about the well-being of their employees and the wider world.

'Greenwashing'

'Greenwashing' is term used to describe practices that appear to be environmentally responsible but aren't. Just because a corporation adopts an image of caring for the environment doesn't mean it actually does. While some consumers may react positively to these types of claims, others see them as stretching the truth.

Customer loyalty

As consumers, millennials are a force to be reckoned with these days. They often prefer to do business with corporations with pro-social messages rather than those just out to make a fast buck. In addition, they are more likely to be loyal to one brand if its corporate values are similar to their personal ones.

Image improvement

A corporation that is socially responsible improves its reputation among consumers who feel good when they buy from companies that are helping their community. It's a win-win situation. They also tend to trust companies that engage in socially responsible practices more than those that do not.

Increased production costs

It can cost a corporation an arm and a leg to be socially responsible. These additional expenses can lead to increased prices of its products for consumers. In the end, it's the consumer who pays the price. Many smaller businesses can be strapped for cash so will find it challenging to do both.

Profits in conflict

The costs of being socially responsible can be high even for large corporations. Their management teams have a duty to shareholders to maximise profits. This can put them between a rock and a hard place. Managers who focus on social responsibility may be replaced by those who favour profits.

Work It Out with Business Idioms   Teaching tool 10.2

Who in your family is a force to be reckoned with? Why?	What's something you own that cost you an arm and a leg?
Have you ever been strapped for cash? What did you do?	What's a good (and legal!) way to make a fast buck?
Describe a time at work when you were in a win-win situation.	Have you ever stretched the truth? What were the circumstances?
Have you ever been between a rock and a hard place? What did you do?	Who is someone you have liked from the get-go? Why?

Who in your family is a force to be reckoned with? Why?	What's something you own that cost you an arm and a leg?
Have you ever been strapped for cash? What did you do?	What's a good (and legal!) way to make a fast buck?
Describe a time at work when you were in a win-win situation.	Have you ever stretched the truth? What were the circumstances?
Have you ever been between a rock and a hard place? What did you do?	Who is someone you have liked from the get-go? Why?

Work It Out with Business Idioms

Teaching tool 11.1

A These leaders are interested in motivating people to see their way of doing things. They inspire others to go the extra mile so that everyone is on the same page.

B These leaders are interested in creating harmony. They want to be everyone's friend and bend over backwards trying to keep everyone happy.

C These leaders are interested in human development. They identify the skills people have so that they can help them to improve those skills down the line.

D These leaders are interested in what others can bring to the table. They value people's ideas and make decisions based on their input.

E These leaders are interested in setting the bar high. They often do tasks themselves to serve as an example to others.

F These leaders are interested in top-down decision-making. They call the shots and expect others to toe the line without questioning orders.

Bend over backwards	Bring (something) to the table
Call the shots	Down the line
Go the extra mile	On the same page
Toe the line	Set the bar high

to work extra hard to do something	to contribute (something) to a group effort
to tell others what to do	at a later date
to do more than what is required	in agreement on how things should be done
to follow the rules without causing trouble	to establish a high standard of quality

Go through something with a fine-toothed comb Words you cannot say: *examine* *hair*	**Have time to kill** Words you cannot say: *period* *nothing*
In the driver's seat Words you cannot say: *car* *control*	**Err on the side of caution** Words you cannot say: *careful* *risk*
Keep one's cool Words you cannot say: *cold* *upset*	**Leave no stone unturned** Words you cannot say: *rock* *move*
Talk someone's ear off Words you cannot say: *speak* *nonstop*	**Up in the air** Words you cannot say: *undecided* *above*

Handouts

Work It Out with Business Idioms — Handout 1.1

F — Martin: Welcome everyone to today's meeting. I hope that you can all see and hear me. As most of you know, my name is Martin Lee. And here with me is Samantha Johnson, our new intern.

B — Paula: Hi Martin and Samantha. Thanks for setting up this meeting. This is Paula Vasquez, here in Barcelona.

H — Lukas: And I'm Lukas Schmidt. I work in the Berlin office, but I'm calling in today from Tokyo. Nice to meet you all!

D — Martin: Thanks, everyone, for making time for today's meeting. So, let's get down to business. I know you all have a lot on your plate these days, so I've only scheduled 30 minutes for this meeting. I assume you've all received today's agenda?

C — Lukas: Um, sorry, but I haven't.

I — Martin: That's fine, Lukas. Basically, I want to discuss our expansion plans into Morocco. Let me quickly get everyone up to speed: Our competitors seem to have money to burn and are planning to expand there as well, so I want to be sure we beat them to the punch. By the way, Samantha, would you mind taking minutes for today's meeting?

E — Samantha: I'd be happy to. I'll share the minutes with the team afterwards.

A — Martin: Great. Thank you, Samantha. The first item on the agenda concerns the timing of our planned expansion. I know you've all been working around the clock to make this happen. Does a spring launch still seem possible?

G — Paula: I don't think spring is going to fly for us here in Spain. I think we'll need until the summer to get everything up and running…

Work It Out with Business Idioms Handout 1.2

	Questions	Answers	Which words…?
1	After the introductions, who suggests that they start working?		
2	Does Martin think that Paula and Lukas have little to do these days?		
3	Does Martin quickly get Paula and Lukas all the information they need?		
4	Do their competitors probably have more or less money than they need?		
5	Does Martin want to achieve something before or after their competitors do?		
6	Have Paula and Lukas been working day and night to make the launch happen?		
7	Does Paula think that a spring launch is going to work for her?		
8	How much time does Paula need for the launch to start operating normally?		

Work It Out with Business Idioms

Handout 1.3

Complete Samantha's notes with the words in the box. Two words are extra and are not used.

| beat | burn | business | clock | fly |
| plate | play | speed | time | up |

Conference call meeting minutes

Present: Martin, Paula (Barcelona), Lukas (Berlin), Samantha

Objective: to discuss expansion plans into Morocco

Time: 30 mins

Martin got down to (1)_____ right away due to short time available for meeting, and the fact everyone has a lot on their (2)_____

Lukas did not have copy of agenda for some reason (check?)

Martin quickly got everyone up to (3)_____ RE Morocco exp. plans, feels the comp has money to (4)_____ – could easily (5)_____ us to the punch

Timing an issue for some, though they've all been working around the (6)_____

Paula says spring's not going to (7)_____ for the launch – needs till summer to get things (8)_____ and running

No follow-up meeting scheduled at this time

Work It Out with Business Idioms Handout 1.4

Match the two parts to make questions. Then, ask and answer the questions.

1. At the moment, do you have a lot on _____?   a   to business

2. When was the last time you had to work around _____?   b   your plate

3. What would you buy if you had some money _____?   c   the punch

4. If you missed several days of class, who would you ask to get you up _____?   d   the clock

5. In meetings, what often happens before everyone gets down _____?   e   fly these days

6. Have you ever planned to do or say something, but then someone else beat you to _____?   f   to speed

7. If your computer broke while you were working from home, who would you call to get it up _____?   g   to burn

8. What is something that people used to do at work, but which doesn't _____?   h   and running

Work It Out with Business Idioms — Handout 2.1

	Questions	Answers
1	What are two examples of 'hard skills'?	
2	What's another name for 'soft skills'?	
3	What are three examples of soft skills?	
4	What's one way to identify your soft skills?	
5	Which types of skills do employers look for?	
6	What does 'transferable skills' mean?	

Circle the meaning (a or b) of each underlined idiom.

1. A rule of thumb that I try to follow is to pay off my credit card each month.

    a) a principle that is based on experience
    b) a principle that works for you but no one else

2. Writing a first draft of your business plan is half the battle.

    a) the easiest part of a task or job
    b) a significant part of the work that is needed

3. It didn't take me long to learn the ropes at my new job.

    a) to learn how to do a task or job
    b) to learn from past mistakes

4. No one volunteered to organise the party, so I decided to step up to the plate.

    a) to do an easy task before a more difficult one
    b) to take responsibility for doing something difficult or unpopular

5. Our deadline is midnight, so I might need some coffee to push me over the finish line.

    a) to delay a goal until you have more time
    b) to make a final effort towards a goal

6. Kenji is a good candidate for the position, but the bottom line is that we need someone with experience.

    a) the least important fact in a situation
    b) the most important fact in a situation

7. I have only a minute, so can you tell me, in a nutshell, what the meeting was about?

    a) in only a few words
    b) in a funny or interesting way

8. Athens is a great choice for our sales meeting as it ticks all the boxes.

    a) to meet all the requirements
    b) to be in a convenient location

Work It Out with Business Idioms

Handout 2.3

Complete the questions with words from the box.
Two words are extra and are not used.

| bottom | half | learn | line | nutshell |
| plate | push | ropes | rule | ticks |

1   What do you want to learn, in a _____, from this class?

2   What do you think is _____ the battle of getting a job?

3   What's a _____ of thumb you have learned from your parents or grandparents?

4   What is the best way to learn the _____ at a new job?

5   What country _____ all the boxes for you as a vacation destination? Why?

6   Describe a time when someone helped _____ you over the finish line. What happened?

7   Describe a time when you stepped up to the _____. What was the outcome?

8   Complete this sentence: The _____ line is that the most important soft skill is teamwork. Do you agree or disagree?

Work It Out with Business Idioms Handout 3.1

	Questions	Answers	Which words…?
1	What do Passive Communicators do when they're asked to help others?		
2	Do Passive Communicators tend to suffer the bad effects of a situation?		
3	Are Aggressive Communicators open or closed about their feelings and intentions?		
4	Do people have a chance to speak when they listen to Aggressive Communicators?		
5	Do people hear and remember all that Passive-aggressive Communicators say?		
6	Do Passive-aggressive Communicators use humour to make what they say clear?		
7	Do Assertive Communicators tend to compromise with others?		
8	Do Assertive Communicators help others right away, or after some time has passed?		

	Find someone who…	Name	Other information
1	gets embarrassed at the drop of a hat		
2	is happy to give another student a hand with their homework		
3	knows someone who makes it hard for others to get a word in edgeways		
4	believes that meeting someone halfway is good business practice		
5	feels they have got the short end of the stick at work		
6	finds it easy to get their point across during class discussions		
7	thinks it's good to put all your cards on the table during negotiations		

Work It Out with Business Idioms   Handout 3.3

Take turns to ask the questions (1–9), stating the four possible responses (a–d).
Circle the letter (a–d) of your partner's responses.

1   You have a work deadline. A coworker stops by to chat. What do you do?

   a) Listen so you don't appear rude.
   b) Tell your coworker to leave because you need to work.
   c) Look at your watch and ask your coworker if it's break time again.
   d) Explain that you have a deadline and suggest catching up later.

2   Someone hands in a report two days late. What do you say?

   a) Nothing.
   b) 'This was due two days ago. Get it done sooner next time.'
   c) 'Are you deaf? Didn't you hear me say the due date?'
   d) 'Thank you. Did you have a problem with the deadline?'

3   You need some help from a coworker so that you can finish a spreadsheet. What do you say?

   a) 'This spreadsheet is taking me a long time to finish.'
   b) 'Get your lazy butt over here and help me.'
   c) 'It would be nice if more people were helpful.'
   d) 'Can you please help me with this spreadsheet?'

4   You disagree with your coworker's idea in a meeting. What do you do?

   a) Smile and say nothing because everyone else likes the idea.
   b) Tell your coworker they're wrong if they think the plan will work.
   c) Ask if your coworker is from another planet since the idea is so strange.
   d) Share your concerns in a clear and respectful way.

5   You're planning to have dinner with a friend after work. Your mother calls and asks you to help her fix her sink right away. What do you do?

   a) Tell your friend you need to reschedule, and then go to your mother's.
   b) Tell your mother you have plans and that she should find someone else.
   c) Tell your mother to call your brother, because he's her favourite.
   d) Tell your mother that you have plans, but say you'll stop by after dinner.

6   You overhear a coworker say that he doesn't like working with you because you're lazy. What do you do?

   a) Nothing, because it's embarrassing.
   b) Tell your coworker to say it to your face.
   c) Act even lazier to teach him a lesson.
   d) Ask your coworker if you can talk later about what you heard.

Work It Out with Business Idioms   Handout 3.3

---

7   Your boss asks for your thoughts on a problematic supplier. What do you say?

       a) 'I'm not sure. What do you think?'
       b) 'They've always been a problem, but that's all we have.'
       c) 'Who chose them? It was probably someone from another department.'
       d) 'I think we should start looking for a new supplier.'

8   Your assistant used double spacing in a report. You asked for single spacing. What do you do?

       a) Redo the report yourself with double spacing.
       b) Set up a meeting with your assistant to discuss the problem.
       c) Ask your assistant, 'Does this look like single spacing?'
       d) Ask your assistant to redo the report with double spacing.

9   A delivery person brings you the wrong food order. What do you do?

       a) Just pay for it and eat it.
       b) Call the restaurant to complain.
       c) Tell the delivery person they should find a new career.
       d) Ask the delivery person if they can bring you the correct order.

Number of 'a' responses: ____

Number of 'b' responses: ____

Number of 'c' responses: ____

Number of 'd' responses: ____

Work It Out with Business Idioms Handout 4.1

Read the six tips. Underline the eight idioms you find.

How to give an elevator pitch

1	**Say who you are**
	This may seem like a no-brainer, but it's important to introduce yourself and say what company you're from and the position you hold. Offer a business card if you have one. Put your best foot forward to make yourself memorable.

2	**Create interest**
	The goal of an elevator pitch is not to overload your audience with details, but to create interest so that they will want to hear more later. You can do this by asking a question, telling a story or sharing a personal experience. Don't let your pitch fall on deaf ears.

3	**Solve a problem**
	Be sure that what you are offering solves a real problem. You want your audience to nod their heads as you speak. If your audience is in the market for something specific, such as a product or service, you will be more likely to keep their attention.

4	**Let your passion show**
	People want to do business with people they like. Smile, make eye contact and let your passion and personality shine through, but don't go overboard. Avoid coming across as fake or insincere.

5	**Keep it short**
	Respect the time of the person you are talking to by keeping your pitch short. Don't beat around the bush. Instead, cut to the chase. Remember, your audience's time is precious.

6	**Practise, practise, practise!**
	It's important to practise your pitch, but you should avoid memorising it. You don't want to sound like a robot. Practise your pitch enough so that you can do it with your eyes closed. Keep things natural and conversational so that you can connect with your audience.

1 _____ = something that is very obvious

2 _____ = to avoid or delay talking about something

3 _____ = to get directly to the main point

4 _____ = to do something very easily

5 _____ = to be ignored by someone

6 _____ = to do something too much

7 _____ = interested in buying something

8 _____ = to make the best impression possible

Work It Out with Business Idioms   Handout 4.2

Student A

Hello, my name is Jessica Hanson. I'm a sales rep at Better Cable Services. Here's my business card. I'm hoping you can give me just a minute of your time, as I'm sure you must be very busy. Are you satisfied with what you pay for this service each year? Perhaps you're in the market for a new cable TV provider? We help hotels around the country find the most cost-effective cable TV plans. That's where I come in. I won't beat around the bush. I'm passionate about helping hotels save money. On average, we save hotels up to 30% on their annual cable bills. I'd love to talk to you about how we can save you big money!

Feedback form 1

The speaker…	Student B	Student C	Student D
says who they are	[ ]	[ ]	[ ]
says which company they work with	[ ]	[ ]	[ ]
says the position they hold	[ ]	[ ]	[ ]
creates interest in the listener	[ ]	[ ]	[ ]
gives the right amount of detail	[ ]	[ ]	[ ]
offers a solution to a problem	[ ]	[ ]	[ ]
comes across as sincere	[ ]	[ ]	[ ]
gets to the point	[ ]	[ ]	[ ]

Feedback form 2

The speaker…	Student B	Student C	Student D
says who they are	[ ]	[ ]	[ ]
says which company they work with	[ ]	[ ]	[ ]
says the position they hold	[ ]	[ ]	[ ]
creates interest in the listener	[ ]	[ ]	[ ]
gives the right amount of detail	[ ]	[ ]	[ ]
offers a solution to a problem	[ ]	[ ]	[ ]
comes across as sincere	[ ]	[ ]	[ ]
gets to the point	[ ]	[ ]	[ ]

Work It Out with Business Idioms   Handout 4.3

Student B

Good afternoon. I'm Gabriel Mendoza and I'm here representing Pure Life Water Filters. Are you familiar with our products? We have recently completed our expansion into northern Europe and we hope you will consider us for your water-filtering needs. It's a no-brainer that people want fresh, clean water, right? Well, all of our products use high-tech materials that keep water clean and free from pollutants. If you have time, feel free to stop by our booth tomorrow in the conference hall. I'd be happy to demonstrate our product so you can see it first-hand. We'll put our best foot forward, and I am sure you will be pleased. Here is my business card in case you wish to get in touch before then. Thanks for your time.

Feedback form 1

The speaker…	Student A	Student C	Student D
says who they are	[ ]	[ ]	[ ]
says which company they work with	[ ]	[ ]	[ ]
says the position they hold	[ ]	[ ]	[ ]
creates interest in the listener	[ ]	[ ]	[ ]
gives the right amount of detail	[ ]	[ ]	[ ]
offers a solution to a problem	[ ]	[ ]	[ ]
comes across as sincere	[ ]	[ ]	[ ]
gets to the point	[ ]	[ ]	[ ]

Feedback form 2

The speaker…	Student A	Student C	Student D
says who they are	[ ]	[ ]	[ ]
says which company they work with	[ ]	[ ]	[ ]
says the position they hold	[ ]	[ ]	[ ]
creates interest in the listener	[ ]	[ ]	[ ]
gives the right amount of detail	[ ]	[ ]	[ ]
offers a solution to a problem	[ ]	[ ]	[ ]
comes across as sincere	[ ]	[ ]	[ ]
gets to the point	[ ]	[ ]	[ ]

Work It Out with Business Idioms   Handout 4.4

Student C

Excuse me. Did you know that demand for high-end Greek food in the UK has grown by over 50% in the past year? Foodies everywhere are looking for a more authentic dining experience, without going overboard on the bill. That's where I come in. Let me cut to the chase. I plan to open a modern Greek restaurant that elevates everyday Greek dishes to something really special. I'm looking for investors who might back my plans, as I'm sure this type of restaurant will be a success. I think my restaurant could even cater events for your business. It would be nice if we could arrange a time to meet to discuss this in more detail.

Feedback form 1

The speaker…	Student A	Student B	Student D
says who they are	[ ]	[ ]	[ ]
says which company they work with	[ ]	[ ]	[ ]
says the position they hold	[ ]	[ ]	[ ]
creates interest in the listener	[ ]	[ ]	[ ]
gives the right amount of detail	[ ]	[ ]	[ ]
offers a solution to a problem	[ ]	[ ]	[ ]
comes across as sincere	[ ]	[ ]	[ ]
gets to the point	[ ]	[ ]	[ ]

Feedback form 2

The speaker…	Student A	Student B	Student D
says who they are	[ ]	[ ]	[ ]
says which company they work with	[ ]	[ ]	[ ]
says the position they hold	[ ]	[ ]	[ ]
creates interest in the listener	[ ]	[ ]	[ ]
gives the right amount of detail	[ ]	[ ]	[ ]
offers a solution to a problem	[ ]	[ ]	[ ]
comes across as sincere	[ ]	[ ]	[ ]
gets to the point	[ ]	[ ]	[ ]

Work It Out with Business Idioms Handout 4.5

Student D

Does this sound familiar? You are rushing to get the kids out the door and off to school. You are also hurrying so you can get to work on time. It's a familiar routine – maybe you even do this with your eyes closed. But then one day you realise that you can't find your car keys. You panic. You ask for help in finding them, but your request falls on deaf ears. Well, this has happened to me more than once. In fact, the average person loses their keys several times a year. We can help with this. We've developed an app that helps you find those lost keys – and other items, too! This app is a real time-saver! I'd love to offer you a free trial as we test our beta version. We are hoping to go to market with the final app in six months.

Feedback form 1

The speaker…	Student A	Student B	Student C
says who they are	[ ]	[ ]	[ ]
says which company they work with	[ ]	[ ]	[ ]
says the position they hold	[ ]	[ ]	[ ]
creates interest in the listener	[ ]	[ ]	[ ]
gives the right amount of detail	[ ]	[ ]	[ ]
offers a solution to a problem	[ ]	[ ]	[ ]
comes across as sincere	[ ]	[ ]	[ ]
gets to the point	[ ]	[ ]	[ ]

Feedback form 2

The speaker…	Student A	Student B	Student C
says who they are	[ ]	[ ]	[ ]
says which company they work with	[ ]	[ ]	[ ]
says the position they hold	[ ]	[ ]	[ ]
creates interest in the listener	[ ]	[ ]	[ ]
gives the right amount of detail	[ ]	[ ]	[ ]
offers a solution to a problem	[ ]	[ ]	[ ]
comes across as sincere	[ ]	[ ]	[ ]
gets to the point	[ ]	[ ]	[ ]

Work It Out with Business Idioms Handout 5.1

Read the information on four different teamwork styles. Some information is missing. Ask your partner questions to complete the missing information.

---

1 The Contributor

Contributors are generally dependable, responsible, organised and reliable. When you have them on your team, you don't have to worry about things getting done. That's because they're thorough and task-oriented, and always have their ducks in a row. They are good at **(1)** _____. They care about **(2)** _____. They are quick to provide their team with information and key data. They will pull out all the stops as needed and will use any resources available in a wise way.

The Contributor

Question: What _____?

Question: What _____?

---

2 The Collaborator

Collaborators are known to be imaginative, forward-looking and goal-oriented, but also flexible.

They are the team members who keep projects things on track. They see the team's mission as the most important thing. They always keep their eye on their prize because they know it's the ultimate goal. Once they set their mind to something, there is no stopping them. They are willing to pitch in and help without being asked. If what the project requires is all hands on deck, they are happy to do their part.

---

3 The Communicator

Communicators are seen as considerate, enthusiastic and supportive, but also relaxed in how they approach and take on team tasks. They tend to go with the flow. They ensure that everything goes smoothly **(3)** _____. This may be anything from conflict management to consensus building. Others view the Communicator **(4)** _____. They offer constructive feedback as needed, but in a respectful, helpful and tactful way.

The Communicator

Question: How _____?

Question: How _____?

---

4 The Challenger

Challengers are often described as direct, outspoken, ethical and honest. They are quick to question why and how things are done. They do not tend to hold their tongue in meetings. They will stick their neck out as required. They are also quick to question the goals and methods, and even the ethics, of the team. This does not mean that they are negative. Rather, they play an important role in keeping things real. They are more willing than others to disagree with the team leader.

Read the information on four different teamwork styles. Some information is missing.
Ask your partner questions to complete the missing information.

---

1 The Contributor

Contributors are generally dependable, responsible, organised and reliable. When you have them on your team, you don't have to worry about things getting done. That's because they're thorough and task-oriented, and always have their ducks in a row. They are good at sharing information with their team members. They care about the details. They are quick to provide their team with information and key data. They will pull out all the stops as needed, and will use any resources available in a wise way.

---

2 The Collaborator

Collaborators are known to be imaginative, forward-looking and goal-oriented, but also flexible.

They are the team members who keep projects things on track. They see the team's mission as **(1)** _____. They always keep their eye on their prize **(2)** _____. Once they set their mind to something, there is no stopping them. They are willing to pitch in and help without being asked. If what the project requires is all hands on deck, they are happy to do their part.

The Collaborator

Question: What _____?

Question: Why _____?

---

3 The Communicator

Communicators are seen as considerate, enthusiastic and supportive, but also relaxed in how they approach and take on team tasks. They tend to go with the flow. They ensure that everything goes smoothly by being an active listener and task facilitator. This may be anything from conflict management to consensus building. Others view the Communicator as a 'people person.' They offer constructive feedback as needed, but in a respectful, helpful, and tactful way.

---

4 The Challenger

Challengers are often described **(3)** _____. They are quick to question why and how things are done. They do not tend to hold their tongue in meetings. They will stick their neck out as required. They are also quick to question the goals and methods, and even the ethics, of the team. This does not mean that they are negative. Rather, they play an important role in keeping things real. They are more willing than others to **(4)** _____.

The Challenger

Question: How _____?

Question: What _____?

Work It Out with Business Idioms Handout 5.3

	Questions	Answers	Which words…?
1	Are Contributors well-prepared for what is going to happen in their team?		
2	Do Contributors tend to quit when things prove to be challenging?		
3	Is the ultimate goal for Collaborators to keep their focus on achieving that goal?		
4	Do Collaborators tend to give something their complete attention and effort?		
5	Do Collaborators sometimes let others do all the work when a project requires everyone's participation?		
6	Are Collaborators or Communicators more likely to happily go along with what everyone else is doing?		
7	Do Challengers keep their thoughts to themselves during meetings?		
8	Are Challengers OK with taking on some risks that others may not?		

Take turns to ask each other these interview-styled questions.

What's your teamwork style?

1	What do you do when a team is formed?	a) Find out what others expect of me b) Better understand our basic mission c) Get to know other team members d) Ask questions about methodology
2	What do you tend to do in meetings?	a) Provide data and other information b) Keep everyone in the team focused c) Make sure everyone is involved d) Raise questions about approaches
3	How would other team members describe you?	a) Factual b) Flexible c) Encouraging d) Direct
4	What are you like most of the time?	a) Hardworking and responsible b) Committed and flexible c) Enthusiastic and humorous d) Authentic and straightforward
5	How would you describe yourself critically?	a) A little short-sighted b) Too focused on results c) Overly laid-back d) Somewhat self-righteous
6	What do you do when your team is in disagreement?	a) Give reasons why one side may be correct b) See it as a basis for changing the team's direction c) Try and break the tension with a joke d) Ask for an open discussion of the issue
7	What do you believe team problem-solving requires?	a) Having good, solid data b) Cooperating with every member c) Having high-level listening skills d) Asking the tough questions
8	What do you consider to be the role of the team leader?	a) To make sure problems are resolved efficiently b) To help the team establish long- and short-term goals c) To create a participatory decision-making climate d) To bring out others' ideas and challenge assumptions
9	What is it about other team members that can annoy you?	a) When they don't complete their tasks on time b) When they don't revisit goals to check progress c) When they don't see the importance of teamwork d) When they don't object to things they disagree with

Work It Out with Business Idioms Handout 6.1

C Caroline: Is everyone here? If so, let's get started. I've set up this meeting today to discuss our third-quarter sales. As you know, sales of our new chocolate bar have dropped by nearly 10% from the second quarter, and we need to do something, and soon. Adam, I don't mean to put you on the spot, but this is your team's account. What has caused sales to decline?

I Adam: It's true that sales have indeed dropped 9.5% worldwide, but if we look closely, we can see that sales remain steady in Europe and the Middle East. In the Americas, they've gone through the roof. But sales are way down in Asia.

E Keiko: That's interesting. Have you been able to determine why sales have dropped there?

D Adam: Yes, I have. It's due to a new chocolate bar that has recently come out of Japan. It's very similar to ours. The company Chico Choco has been advertising it throughout East Asia, and it's taken the region by storm.

H Caroline: But why would their chocolate bar cut into our sales?

A Adam: Well, although our products are similar, our marketing campaigns are completely different. We have TV and print ads, like Chico Choco does, but they are much stronger in their social media ads than we are.

J Keiko: In what way? Don't we also advertise on social media?

G Adam: Yes, we do, but our ads aren't really up to scratch, in my opinion. Their campaigns have focused on users creating 30-second videos of themselves dancing happily while they eat their chocolate bar. These are really popular.

B Keiko: So, they dance to music?

K Adam: Yes, and I think that's why it's been so successful. Chico Choco has its own song that repeats the product name ten times in just 30 seconds.

F Caroline: Thank you, Adam. I think you really hit the nail on the head on why they've succeeded. So, we clearly need to step up our game there. We can't copy the dance idea, of course, but we can come up with something creative if we think outside the box. Let's view some of their videos and then rack our brains to see if we can come up with something.

Work It Out with Business Idioms Handout 6.2

	Questions	Answers	Which words…?
1	Who first asks Adam a question that's difficult to answer?		
2	Have sales gone up or down in the Americas?		
3	Has Chico Choco's new chocolate bar quickly become popular in East Asia?		
4	Does Adam think his company's social media ads are good enough?		
5	Does Caroline think Adam describes exactly why Chico Choco succeeded?		
6	Does Caroline think their company needs to improve its performance?		
7	Does Caroline think they should copy Chico Choco's chocolate bar quickly, or think of their own solution in a more creative way?		
8	Does Caroline suggest that they think very hard or take a break after viewing some videos?		

Work It Out with Business Idioms   Handout 6.3

Complete the questions with words from the box.
Two words are extra and are not used.

box	nail	rack	roof	scratch
seat	spot	step	storm	work

1. What's a product whose sales have gone through the _____ this year? Can you explain why?

2. When was the last time you had to _____ your brains to come up with a solution to a problem?

3. Has your boss ever put you on the _____? What were the circumstances?

4. What's an example of a viral video that has taken the online community by _____?

5. What's an example of an item you purchased that you later found was not up to _____? What did you do about it?

6. Do you remember a time when someone in a meeting was asked a question and they really hit the _____ on the head with their response?

7. When was the last time you had to _____ up your game to complete a project or assignment?

8. What are three possible uses for a paper clip, besides being used to hold paper together? Think outside the _____ and come up with creative uses.

Work It Out with Business Idioms   Handout 6.4

Come up with some marketing ideas for a new product.

Your company produces many types of traditional soft drinks, but, lately, sales of its last three offerings have not exactly gone through the roof. Your latest product is called *Swarm*. It is an all-natural energy drink that, among its ingredients, contains several types of powdered, edible insects. The company feels that this will be its biggest selling point and that the product could take the soft-drinks world by storm. As members of the marketing team, your boss has asked you to rack your brains to come up with some creative ideas for marketing the product.

Use these questions to guide your discussion.

- What group do you think will be the primary market for the product?
- What group could be a secondary market for the product?
- What are the best ways to reach these markets?

Consider these possible marketing strategies, or come up with your own ideas. Then, take notes below on your ideas. Be prepared to share your ideas with the class.

Influencer marketing	Partner marketing	User-generated marketing
Cause marketing	Telemarketing	Free sample marketing
Event marketing	Direct mail marketing	email marketing
Freebie marketing	Tradeshow marketing	Social media marketing

Notes

Work It Out with Business Idioms   Handout 7.1

Read the text. Then, work together to determine which sentence (a–e) goes into each gap (1–5).

a) Consider what impact the decision may have when you make your choice.
b) It's useful to write the possible solutions down so you have a record.
c) Write up a detailed plan for implementing the solution.
d) Gather the information you need to define the problem.
e) Consider what you and others need to do to solve each problem.

How to solve a problem

1 Identify the details of the problem

(1)_____ There may be more than meets the eye. Consider the reasons for the problem – workplace rules and procedures, employee roles and responsibilities, and so on. It's a good idea to write down the outcome you want, but don't assume what the solution should be at this point.

2 Brainstorm solutions

Think about and discuss every possible solution you can think of. If possible, brainstorm with various people who are affected by the problem so that you can get a larger understanding of what might need to be done. (2)_____ Don't throw cold water on any idea. At this stage in the game, don't worry if the ideas are good or bad.

3 Evaluate the solutions

Look at all the possible solutions and evaluate each one. You may feel overwhelmed by all the choices, but this is par for the course. Ask yourself which problems are easy to solve, and which are more difficult. Think about the resources that are available for each one.
(3)_____

4 Make a decision

Once you have considered all the possible solutions and narrowed them down, it's time to decide on one solution. This is a piece of cake for some people, but others will struggle to make a firm decision. Be sure that the solution clearly addresses the root cause of the problem.
(4)_____

5 Take action

(5)_____ Don't bite off more than you can chew – be sure that your plan is feasible. Get any necessary approvals and then put your plan into action. Finally, cross your fingers and hope your solution solves the problem!

Work It Out with Business Idioms   Handout 7.2

	Questions	Answers	Which words…?
1	When you look at a problem, is there sometimes more to it than what may appear at first?		
2	Should you say that an idea is bad during the brainstorming process?		
3	Is it normal to feel overwhelmed by a large number of possible solutions?		
4	Does everyone find it challenging to decide on a solution?		
5	When it's time to take action, is it a good idea to try and do more than you're capable of?		
6	Do you implement your plan before or after you get any necessary approvals?		
7	Is there something you can do to show that you hope for good luck?		

Work It Out with Business Idioms   Handout 7.3

Circle the meaning (a or b) of each underlined idiom.

1   If something is <u>a piece of cake</u>, it's very _____ to do.

    a) easy
    b) difficult

2   If you don't know something <u>at this stage of the game</u>, you don't know it _____.

    a) at this point in the process
    b) because the rules are unclear

3   When you <u>bite off more than you can chew</u>, you _____.

    a) learn more and more every year
    b) do more than you're capable of

4   You <u>cross your fingers</u> when you want _____ luck.

    a) bad
    b) good

5   If there is <u>more than meets the eye</u>, there is _____.

    a) more than there appears to be at first
    b) more positive than negative information

6   Something that is <u>par for the course</u> is _____.

    a) normal
    b) not normal

7   If you <u>put</u> a plan <u>into action</u>, you _____ it.

    a) start or implement
    b) delay or cancel

8   When you <u>throw cold water on</u> an idea, you are _____ about the idea.

    a) positive
    b) negative

Work It Out with Business Idioms Handout 8.1

Building a global brand

If you want to build a global brand, you will need to do more than have a great product and a catchy slogan. You'll need to learn the ins and outs of the culture you are selling into. These four tips may be useful in helping you launch your branch across borders.

1	**Study consumers' behaviour** A consumer may have certain purchasing preferences in one culture, but that doesn't mean they are universal. When Walmart built its stores in China, it expected to hit pay dirt. The company built all its stores near industrial parks. It didn't realise that Chinese consumers prefer to shop near home, not near work.
2	**Think broadly** A company may one day wish to expand on what it sells, so it's important that a company's name is broad enough. As the company Boston Chicken expanded its offering into products other than poultry, their name no longer cut the mustard. So it changed its name to Boston Market. It was a smart move and the company came up smelling like roses.
3	**Be culturally sensitive** It's essential to create culturally appropriate ads that appeal to international customers. The luxury brand Dolce & Gabbana once got into hot water for its ad campaign in China. The ad showed a Chinese woman trying to eat Italian food with chopsticks while a male voice gave her instructions. The Chinese government criticised the ad and sales took a nosedive.
4	**Check any translations** A great name in one language may translate into something confusing, embarrassing or even offensive in another. The French cheese brand Kiri had to change its name to Kibi at the eleventh hour when it was getting ready to launch the product in Iran. That's because it realised that 'kiri' in Farsi means 'rotten'. The company definitely would have had egg on its face if it hadn't made the name change!

1 _____ = dropped quickly

2 _____ = got into trouble

3 _____ = appeared foolish

4 _____ = at the latest possible moment

5 _____ = the particular details of a situation

6 _____ = make a lot of money quickly

7 _____ = was adequate enough

8 _____ = emerged from a difficult situation successfully

Work It Out with Business Idioms Handout 8.2

	Questions	Answers	Which words…?
1	Is it more important to have a general understanding of another culture, or the full details?		
2	Did Walmart expect to struggle in China for a while, or make money quickly?		
3	When Boston Chicken expanded, was its name a problem?		
4	Was the result of Boston Chicken's name change positive or negative?		
5	Did Dolce and Gabbana get into trouble for its ad in China?		
6	Did Dolce and Gabbana's sales in China go up because of its ad campaign?		
7	Did the company Kiri change its name in Iran right away?		
8	How would Kiri have appeared if it hadn't made the name change?		

Work It Out with Business Idioms   Handout 9.1

K   Customer: Hello.

C   Service agent: Hello. I'm calling from Ace Cable Services. I'm just following up on your recent purchase of our cable TV subscription programme. I wanted to see if you were satisfied with your order.

I   Customer: Yes, I'm very pleased. It was installed on time and everything seems to be working fine. They came a little early, but I was home, so that was fine.

G   Service agent: I'm pleased to hear that. Here at Ace Cable Services, we pride ourselves on being ahead of the curve in what we offer our most loyal customers. We want to be sure that customers are happy with our products and receive bang for their buck. Would you be willing to take a short online survey for us?

A   Customer: Um, sure, as long as the survey doesn't take too long.

M   Service agent: Great, thank you. You should receive an email shortly with a link to our survey. Once it's completed, you will receive a coupon for a free movie channel of your choice, no strings attached. Again, thank you for your time. Goodbye.

E   Customer: No problem. Goodbye.

J   Service agent: Good morning. Genesis Cosmetics. Can I help you?

D   Customer: Hi, I'm so glad that I have finally got hold of you. I've been waiting for 30 minutes and I'm almost at the end my rope. I'm calling about some face cream that I recently purchased online from your company. To cut a long story short, the package arrived yesterday, but it has the wrong face cream in it. My purchase order number is 299140.

N   Service agent: Let me just pull that information up so I can get to the bottom of this. Yes, I found it. You purchased two jars of the Omega Face Cream?

H   Customer: That's correct, but I received two jars of the Matsudo cream.

B   Service agent. I'm so sorry, I'll get the ball rolling on that right away and I'll arrange to have your original order sent out today. Feel free to keep the Omega Face Cream. There's no need to return it. Is there anything else I can help you with?

L   Customer: No, you've been very helpful. Thank you.

F   Service agent. You're welcome. Goodbye, and thank you for being part of the Genesis Cosmetics family.

Work It Out with Business Idioms Handout 9.2

Choose the correct answer choice (a or b) for each question.

1. Which company do you think is <u>ahead of the curve</u> regarding its use of technology?

    a) in need of financial investment
    b) ahead of current thinking or trends

2. Describe a time at work when you felt as if you were <u>at the end of your rope</u>.

    a) having no strength or patience left
    b) being recognised for an achievement

3. What are some ways to <u>get hold of</u> a customer these days?

    a) to manage to contact someone
    b) to help someone in need

4. Have you recently purchased a product that offered you a lot of <u>bang for your buck</u>?

    a) reasons for exchanging an item
    b) good value for money

5. What would you be happy to do for your friends, with <u>no strings attached</u>?

    a) having no conditions or expectations in an agreement
    b) having a good time doing something even if others aren't

6. If someone stole your identity, what would you first try to do to <u>get to the bottom of it</u>?

    a) to find an explanation for something
    b) to accept that you are in a bad position

7. At the beginning of a sales meeting, what's one way to <u>get the ball rolling</u>?

    a) to involve people who are usually not active
    b) to do something that starts an activity

8. <u>To cut a long story short</u>, how did you get your job?

    a) to explain what happened in a few words
    b) to make a story more interesting than it really is

Work It Out with Business Idioms   Handout 9.3

Replace the crossed out words with an idiom from the lesson.
Then, write a response to each review.

☆☆☆☆☆

This company is awesome! I'm not someone who usually writes reviews but they are way ~~ahead of current thinking and trends~~ (1)_____ in how they offer ~~good value for money~~ (2)_____. I had one small issue and contacted their Customer Service department. They resolved my problem immediately. I have been a loyal customer for many years and will continue to be one. Thank you, and keep it up!

[response box]

☆☆☆☆☆

This company has a pretty good loyalty programme. I'm a Silver member and they just made it easier to achieve Gold status this year. They also now send out coupons that you can use anytime, anywhere, ~~having no conditions or expectations in an agreement~~ (3)_____. I had an issue with a recent purchase and they were able to ~~find an explanation for~~ (4)_____ the problem in just two minutes.

[response box]

☆☆☆☆☆

This company seems to have gone downhill in recent months. I had to call Customer Service recently and it took forever for me to ~~manage to contact~~ someone (5)_____. They transferred me to another department and, to ~~explain what happened in a few words~~ (6)_____, they cut me off! I'm at the end my rope and I have no idea what to do now. This company does not care about its customers.

[response box]

	How to Build Customer Loyalty	You	Pair	Group
1	**Be great at what you do** A simple way to build customer loyalty is to simply be the best out there.			
2	**Have the right employees** Employees who buy into the company's values are more likely to share their excitement with others.			
3	**Know your customers** Set up a database with important information about your customers.			
4	**Don't rely too much on technology** You may think this makes you ahead of the curve, but customers get frustrated if they can't get hold of a company representative.			
5	**Set up a reward system** This is one of the best ways for loyal customers to get bang for their buck.			
6	**Encourage customer reviews** Positive reviews will drive others to your business. Negative reviews can help you find ways to improve.			

Work It Out with Business Idioms Handout 10.1

Take notes on each text's key ideas.

Corporate Social Responsibility (CSR)	
Advantages	Disadvantages

Read the text. Underline the eight idioms you find and complete the definitions below.

Advantages of Corporate Social Responsibility

Image improvement

A corporation that is socially responsible improves its reputation among consumers who feel good when they buy from companies that are helping their community. It's a win-win situation. They also tend to trust companies that engage in socially responsible practices more than those that do not.

Employee satisfaction

The way a corporation treats its community says a lot about how it treats its employees. Corporations with a strong commitment to social responsibility from the get-go find it easier to find and retain employees. People want to work for companies that care about the well-being of their employees and the wider world.

Customer loyalty

As consumers, millennials are a force to be reckoned with these days. They often prefer to do business with corporations with pro-social messages rather than those just out to make a fast buck. In addition, they are more likely to be loyal to one brand if its corporate values are similar to their personal ones.

Disadvantages of Corporate Social Responsibility

Increased production costs

It can cost a corporation an arm and a leg to be socially responsible. These additional expenses can lead to increased prices of its products for consumers. In the end, it's the consumer who pays the price. Many smaller businesses can be strapped for cash so will find it challenging to do both.

Profits in conflict

The costs of being socially responsible can be high even for large corporations. Their management teams have a duty to shareholders to maximise profits. This can put them between a rock and a hard place. Managers who focus on social responsibility may be replaced by those who favour profits.

'Greenwashing'

'Greenwashing' is term used to describe practices that appear to be environmentally responsible but aren't. Just because a corporation adopts an image of caring for the environment doesn't mean it actually does. While some consumers may react positively to these types of claims, others see them as stretching the truth.

1 _____ = from the very beginning
2 _____ = be very expensive
3 _____ = earn money quickly and easily
4 _____ = have little or no money at the moment
5 _____ = a situation that is good for everyone involved
6 _____ = a person or thing that is strong and powerful
7 _____ = in a situation with two equally bad alternatives
8 _____ = saying something that's not exactly true (to improve a situation)

Work It Out with Business Idioms Handout 10.3

	Questions	Answers	Which words...?
1	Who wins when a corporation improves its reputation as a result of its approach to corporate social responsibility?		
2	Do socially responsible corporations find it easier to keep employees if they start their CSR efforts early?		
3	Do millennials have much power these days?		
4	Do millennials often prefer to do business with corporations that earn money quickly and easily?		
5	Does it cost much money for a corporation to be socially responsible?		
6	What don't small businesses often have enough of?		
7	Do management teams that only focus on increasing profits for shareholders find themselves in a good position?		
8	Are corporations that engage in 'greenwashing' being honest?		

Work It Out with Business Idioms

Handout 10.4

Ask and answer questions with your partner to complete the information.

Student A

Corporate Social Responsibility

1 The toy company Lego has reduced the amount of packaging it uses and has started using more sustainable materials in its production processes. It has also invested heavily in _____ [What?].

2 The shoe company TOMS is not all about making a fast buck. Instead, it gives a third of its net profits to charities that support physical and mental health. The company also supports various educational initiatives.

3 Johnson & Johnson has reduced its carbon footprint _____ [How?]. The company also works to provide clean, safe water to many communities. It's win-win situation for all involved.

4 The coffee chain Starbucks has a socially responsible hiring process that aims to diversify its workforce. They hire veterans, refugees, and people who are looking to start their careers.

5 Google is a force to be reckoned with. The tech giant has invested in renewable energy sources. The company also is known for _____ [What?].

6 The streaming giant Netflix offers benefits to support its employees. The company offers 52 weeks of paid time off to new parents. This compares favourably to 18 weeks offered by other tech companies.

7 The outdoor-clothing company Patagonia works with many factories to produce clothes that don't cost an arm and a leg. The company has insisted _____ [For how long?] that its employees receive a wage that is above the minimum wage.

8 The drug company Pfizer focuses on 'corporate citizenship', with initiatives including the spreading of awareness about diseases and provision of health care to women who may be strapped for cash.

Work It Out with Business Idioms　　　　　　　　　　　　　　　　　　　　Handout 10.5

Ask and answer questions with your partner to complete the information.　　　　　　　　　　　Student B

Corporate Social Responsibility

1. The toy company Lego has reduced the amount of packaging it uses and has started using more sustainable materials in its production processes. It has also invested heavily in alternative energy sources.

2. The shoe company TOMS is not all about making a fast buck. Instead, it gives _____ [How much?] of its net profits to charities that support physical and mental health. The company also supports

3. Johnson & Johnson has reduced its carbon footprint by investing in cleaner energy. The company also works to provide clean, safe water to many communities. It's win-win situation for all involved.

4. The coffee chain Starbucks has a socially responsible hiring process that aims to diversify its workforce. They hire _____ [Who?].

5. Google is a force to be reckoned with. The tech giant has invested in renewable energy sources. The company also is known for standing up against discrimination.

6. The streaming giant Netflix offers benefits to support its employees. The company offers _____ [How many?] weeks of paid time off to new parents. This compares favourably to 18 weeks offered by other tech companies.

7. The outdoor-clothing company Patagonia works with many factories to produce clothes that don't cost an arm and a leg. The company has insisted from the get-go that its employees receive a wage that is above the minimum wage.

8. The drug company Pfizer focuses on '_____' [What?], with initiatives including the spreading of awareness about diseases and provision of health care to women who may be strapped for cash.

Work It Out with Business Idioms Handout 11.1

Write the information alongside the appropriate letter.

A		
B		
C		
D		
E		
F		

Work It Out with Business Idioms Handout 11.2

	Questions	Answers	Which words…?
1	Do Visionary leaders want people to do just enough, or more than is necessary?		
2	Do Visionary leaders expect people to be in agreement on how things should be done?		
3	Do Affiliative leaders work extra hard to keep people happy?		
4	Are Coaching leaders more interested in people's past or future development?		
5	Are Democratic leaders interested in what other people can contribute?		
6	What level of quality do Pace-setting leaders expect from others?		
7	Do Commanding leaders let others make important decisions?		
8	Do Commanding leaders want others to follow the rules they set, or break them?		

Work It Out with Business Idioms Handout 11.3

Circle the meaning (a or b) of each underlined idiom.

1. My team is always ready to go the extra mile to make sure our projects succeed.

    a) to do more than what is required
    b) to do less than what is required

2. We can't move forward until everyone is on the same page.

    a) present at a meeting
    b) in agreement on how things should be done

3. The servers bend over backwards to make sure our experience is positive.

    a) to break all the rules
    b) to work extra hard to do something

4. We can't say what will happen to our agreement down the line.

    a) without your input
    b) at a later date

5. I have no idea what Jason can bring to the table.

    a) to contribute something to a group effort
    b) to include everyone in a discussion

6. Be sure to set the bar high if you want to get the most out of your employees.

    a) to establish a high standard of quality
    b) to offer a very large salary

7. Our opinions are valuable, but it's the directors here who call the shots.

    a) to get input from key players
    b) to tell others what to do

8. If you want our boss to like you, I suggest that you toe the line.

    a) to ask questions when you don't understand
    b) to follow the rules without causing trouble

Work It Out with Business Idioms   Handout 11.4

	Which type of leader are you?	Student 1	Student 2	Student 3	You
1	What's the role of a leader? a) To find agreement through participation b) To set high performance standards c) To insist that people do things their way d) To get others to see their vision e) To create emotional bonds f) To develop people for the future				
2	What's the most important quality in a leader? a) Collaborative working style b) Results-oriented c) Authority d) Self-confidence e) Team building f) Self-awareness				
3	Which of the following best describes your leadership style? a) 'What do *you* think?' b) 'Follow my lead.' c) 'Do exactly what I tell you.' d) 'Come with me on a journey.' e) 'People come first.' f) 'Why don't you try this?'				
4	Which leader do you identify most with? a) U.S. President Abraham Lincoln b) SpaceX founder Elon Musk c) Former British prime minister Margaret Thatcher d) Apple founder Steve Jobs e) Talk show host Ellen DeGeneres f) Indian leader Mahatma Gandhi				

Work It Out with Business Idioms Handout 12.1

Complete the interview tips with words from the box.
Four words are extra and are not used.

| air   book   caution   chair   comb   cool |
| ear   hand   man   seat   stone   time |

Do's	Don'ts
Find out about the company and interviewer in advance. Leave no (1)_____ unturned. Dress appropriately for the position. Err on the side of (2)_____ and dress conservatively. Know the exact time and location of your interview, including how long it takes to get there and who the contact person is. Arrive at least ten minutes before your interview start time. If you have (3)_____ to kill beforehand, use it to relax. Treat other people you meet while at the company with courtesy and respect. They might be asked about you as part of the hiring process. Be sure that you understand your interviewer's name and its correct pronunciation. Address your interviewer by title and last name. Respond to questions clearly. Be thorough in your responses while at the same time being concise in your wording. Be sure that you understand the hiring process. Don't leave the next steps up in the (4)_____.	Don't send in a CV that contains errors. Go through it with a fine-toothed (5)_____ before sending it in. Don't try to take over the interview. Let the interviewer be in the driver's (6)_____. Don't make negative comments about your previous or current employers. Don't talk the interviewer's (7)_____ off. Sharing long stories or irrelevant information can distract from your qualifications and the overall impression you make. Don't exaggerate your experience or qualifications. Never lie or mislead during the interview. Don't be a comedian. Be pleasant, but remember that the interviewing process is formal and serious. Don't ask about salary and benefits unless these are brought up by the employer. Don't act desperate, as though you would take any job that is offered. Don't exhibit nervousness or frustration. Keep your (8)_____, even when asked difficult or uncomfortable questions.

Work It Out with Business Idioms — Handout 12.2

	Questions	Answers	Which words…?
1	Before an interview, should you do everything you can to find out about the company?		
2	Should you take a risk when you dress for an interview?		
3	What should you do ten minutes before your interview is scheduled to begin?		
4	Is it good to leave things unresolved regarding the next steps in the interview process?		
5	Is it necessary to examine your CV very closely before you send it in?		
6	Who should be in control of the interview – you or the interviewer?		
7	During the interview, should you keep talking and talking to the interviewer?		
8	Is it better to be calm, animated, or evasive when the interviewer asks you a difficult question?		

Work It Out with Business Idioms Handout 12.3

You work for a trendy fashion boutique. You are going to interview four people for the position of Social Media Manager. Write five questions you would like to ask a potential hire.

Student A

	Interviewer questions	Candidate 1	Candidate 2	Candidate 3	Candidate 4
1					
2					
3					
4					
5					

Work It Out with Business Idioms Handout 12.4

You work for a small regional airline. You are going to interview four people for the position of Flight Attendant. Write five questions you would like to ask a potential hire.

Student B

	Interviewer questions	Candidate 1	Candidate 2	Candidate 3	Candidate 4
1					
2					
3					
4					
5					

Idiom dictionary

A force to be reckoned with – a person or thing that is strong and powerful

> A. *The new board member is young and seems to lack experience.*
> B. *Don't be fooled by appearances. He's **a force to be reckoned with** in the boardroom.*

A new study explains why women in their 40s, 50s and beyond are considered **a force to be reckoned with** in the workplace.

A no-brainer – something that is very obvious

> A. *It was smart to promote Jan from assistant manager to manager.*
> B. *I agree. It was **a no-brainer**.*

Installing solar energy at your place of business is **a no-brainer**. It reduces energy costs and provides long-term price stability.

A piece of cake – a very easy task

> A. *I'm worried about tomorrow's job interview.*
> B. *Don't worry. It will be **a piece of cake** for you. You have all the skills they need.*

Any students who have tried to create a bibliography or a reference list know that it's not **a piece of cake**.

Origin: The idiom may have originated in the 1870s when cake was often given as a prize for winning a competition.

A rule of thumb – a principle that is based on experience

> A. *Should I address people at my new job by their first names, or should I be more formal?*
> B. *A good **rule of thumb** is to wait until they invite you to call them by their first names.*

A good **rule of thumb** is that you should save at least 10% of your income for retirement.

Origin: The idiom is believed to date back to the 1600s when accurate measuring tools were not available in England. A builder's thumb would typically be used to give an approximate measurement.

Idiom dictionary

A win-win situation – a situation that is good for everyone involved

>   A. *Do you think it's a good idea for our company to adopt a 'flexible hours' programme?*
>   B. *Absolutely. It's **a win-win situation** for both employer and employee.*

Hiring students as consultants for start-ups is **a win-win situation**. The start-ups get extra help, and the students get a look behind the scenes at a new company.

Variation: a win-win solution; a win-win strategy

Ahead of the curve – ahead of current thinking or trends

>   A. *Her ideas are very innovative.*
>   B. *Yes, she's very much **ahead of the curve**. She may be running the company someday.*

The company's president said that we need to get **ahead of the curve** on our climate challenges in order to remain sustainable and continue to thrive.

Origin: The idiom may stem from the shape of a bell curve. If you are ahead of the bell graph's curve, you are staying ahead of everything else.

All hands on deck – everyone is needed

>   A. *The director wants our team's report by 5pm today.*
>   B. *So, it's going be **all hands on deck** for the rest of the day.*

It was **all hands on deck** to restore power in Alabama after Hurricane Zeta hit.

Origin: The idiom was originally a naval expression. A ship's captain would call for **all hands** (sailors) **on deck** (a part of a ship) to help during an emergency.

At the drop of a hat – immediately and without delay

>   A. *Who should I talk to if I need help with this?*
>   B. *I'd call Lucy in IT. She can usually come and help **at the drop of a hat**.*

Workers now need to shift roles **at the drop of a hat**, and that requires training in new skills, processes and technology.

Origin: The idiom probably dates back to the 19th century, when a man would signal the start of a race or contest by grabbing his hat and thrusting it towards the ground.

At the eleventh hour – at the latest possible moment

    A. *Did they submit their proposal in time?*
    B. *Yes, they did it **at the eleventh hour**, just minutes before the deadline.*

The blood cancer survivor who found a donor **at the eleventh hour** is highlighting the importance of stem-cell donations.

At the end of one's rope – (US) having no strength or patience left

    A. *I'm worried about Matt. He's been **at the end of his rope** for weeks.*
    B. *I think it may be time for him to look for another job.*

As a single parent, he was **at the end of his rope** trying to keep some normalcy in his young son's life.

Origin: The idiom derives from tying a rope around the neck of a domesticated animal, limiting its movement. By doing this, the animal could graze on grass only as far as the rope allowed.

Variation: to reach the end of one's rope; at the end of one's tether (UK)

At this stage of the game – at this point in the process or situation

    A. *Do you think now is a good time to sell stock?*
    B. ***At this stage of the game** I would have to say no.*

'**At this stage of the game**,' the fire chief said, 'I wouldn't even want to guess what caused the fire.'

Bang for one's buck – (US) good value for money

    A. *Which of these speakers do you think I should buy?*
    B. *This one's a little more expensive, but its additional features offer you more **bang for your buck**.*

To no one's surprise, Florida is the US state in which your retirement dollars will get you the most **bang for your buck**.

Origin: The idiom has been in use since the 1950s, when the US Army suggested that a stockpile of nuclear weapons (bang) was better value (buck) than a large army. The word 'buck' is a slang word meaning 'dollar.'

Beat around the bush – to avoid or delay talking about something

 A. *I really don't how to say this.*
 B. *Don't **beat around the bush**. Just tell me.*

Let's not **beat around the bush**. The country's future looks grim and young people are looking for opportunities overseas.

Origin: The idiom comes from a 15th-century hunting practice in which rich hunters hired 'beaters' to drive birds and small animals out of bushes so that the hunters could easily get to them. The beaters would use sticks to beat around the bushes to force the animals out.

Beat (someone) to the punch – to achieve something before someone else does

 A. *Did you suggest your slogan idea to your boss in today's meeting?*
 B. *I was planning to, but Sandra raised her hand first and **beat me to the punch**.*

By the time the company announced that it was adding the new technology across its latest lineup of mobile phones, much of its competition had already **beaten them to the punch**.

Origin: The idiom comes from the sport of boxing, where the winner beats their opponent by delivering a final punch resulting in a knockout.

Bend over backwards – to work extra hard to do something

 A. *There is a lot of competition in the travel industry these days.*
 B. *Many companies are **bending over backwards** to hang on to their existing customers.*

The street vendor wears a Spider-Man suit every day. He's **bending over backwards** to make a sale.

Between a rock and a hard place – in a situation with two equally bad alternatives

A. I'm really unhappy in my job, but I can't afford to quit right now.
B. It sounds like you're **between a rock and a hard place**.

The software company was left with no good options. They were clearly stuck **between a rock and a hard place**.

Origin: The idiom comes from ancient Greek mythology. In Homer's *Odyssey*, Odysseus must sail between a monster that lives on cliffs (a rock) and a dangerous whirlpool (a hard place).

Variation: stuck between a rock and a hard place; caught between a rock and a hard place

Bite off more than one can chew – to do more than one is capable of

A. I asked for it, but I don't feel I can manage all the additional responsibilities that my boss gave me.
B. It seems to me that you may have **bitten off more than you can chew**.

The government decided to take a leading role in shaping Middle East policy, but they may have **bitten off more than they can chew**.

Bring (something) to the table – to contribute something to a group effort

A. Do you think Omar was a good choice for regional manager?
B. I do. He **brings years of experience to the table**.

Reviewers were quick to criticise the romantic comedy because it didn't **bring anything fresh to table**.

Call the shots – to tell others what to do

A. Do you think Amanda will approve my transfer?
B. It's not really up to Amanda. Claire is the one who **calls the shots** around here.

While the former CEO cannot **call the shots**, he will likely continue to have a large influence on day-to-day activities.

Origin: One theory is that the idiom comes from the game of billiards, where a player has to say (call) where the ball will go (the shot). Another theory is that it comes from the game of darts, where the thrower has to call out the exact spot where the dart is expected to land.

Idiom dictionary

Come up smelling like roses – to emerge from a difficult situation successfully

    A. *I heard that everyone except Tom lost money in last year's real estate deal.*
    B. *It's true. He **came up smelling like roses** because he refused to sell, and now his investment is worth double what it was.*

Why does the little guy always get hurt, and the big guy **comes up smelling like roses**?

Variation: come up/out smelling like a rose/roses/of roses

Cost (someone) an arm and a leg – to be very expensive

    A. *Why didn't you join your friends on their vacation to Tahiti?*
    B. *I wanted to, but the trip would have ended up **costing me and arm and a leg**.*

While electric cars can be on the pricy side, recharging them won't **cost you an arm and a leg**.

Cross your fingers – to hope for good luck

    A. *Did you submit your proposal?*
    B. *I did. Now I can only **cross my fingers** and hope that it gets accepted.*

With this latest hurricane forecast, let's **cross our fingers** that it doesn't make landfall.

Origin: The act of crossing one's fingers goes back 2,000 years. The people in northern Europe at that time would cross their fingers to form a cross, a symbol of good luck.

Cut the mustard – to be adequate enough (often used in the negative)

    A. *The temporary employee you sent over this morning just isn't **cutting the mustard**.*
    B. *I'm very sorry to hear that. I'll send over a more experienced temp tomorrow.*

I tried cooking a plant-based burger instead of a beef burger and, frankly, the plant-based burger didn't **cut the mustard**.

Cut to the chase – to get directly to the main point

    A. *What did you do after you greeted your guests?*
    B. *We **cut to the chase** and began our negotiation.*

If you're not up to reading the full review, you can **cut to the chase** and go directly to the summary.

Origin: The idiom dates back to the silent movie era, when films often ended in chase scenes. A director would sometimes want to get to the more exciting chase scene quickly so as not to bore the audience.

Do something with one's eyes closed – to do something very easily

    A. *Did you do any hiking when you were in Thailand?*
    B. *Yes, but with a guide. He knew the route through the forest so well that he could probably **do it with his eyes closed**.*

Isobel set up the product display in record time. It was such a simple task that she could **do it with her eyes closed**.

Down the line – at a later date

    A. *Do you have any plans to go back to graduate school?*
    B. *I don't have any immediate plans, but **down the line** – who knows?*

The new auto loans may be problematic for banks **down the line**.

Err on the side of caution – to be especially careful rather than take a risk

    A. *What time do you want to go to the airport?*
    B. *Let's **err on the side of caution** and leave soon. The traffic could be bad.*

Due to the flu outbreak, the daycare centre chose to **err on the side of caution** and close down for a week.

Fall on deaf ears – to be ignored by someone

    A. *Did you get a chance to tell the committee about your privacy concerns?*
    B. *Yes, but I think what I said largely **fell on deaf ears**. I doubt anything will change.*

The opposition leader's call for post-election protests has **fallen on deaf ears**.

From the get-go – (US) from the very beginning

   A. *How is your work on the Miller account coming along?*
   B. *Not great. That account has been a problem **from the get-go**.*

The salon and spa owner said that owning her own business was her goal **from the get-go**.

Variation: from the word go (UK)

Get a word in edgeways – to have a chance to speak

   A. *Layla completely dominated today's staff meeting.*
   B. *You can say that again! It was impossible for anyone to **get a word in edgeways**.*

Too many virtual meeting attendees means that it's difficult for some participants to **get a word in edgeways**.

Origin: The word *edgeways* refers to turning something on its side (or edge) in order to insert it into a small space. The idiom suggests that one must put one's words edgeways in order to squeeze them into a conversation.

Variation: get a word in edgewise

Get down to business – to start working

   A. *I think everyone is now here, Ms. Walters.*
   B. *Oh, thank you, Dan. All right everyone, let's **get down to business**.*

After taking Monday off, the city council **got down to business**, starting with the approval of several zoning requests.

Get hold of (someone) – to manage to contact someone

   A. *Do you know how to **get hold of Marcus**?*
   B. *I don't have his phone number, but here's his email address.*

The bank is trying to **get hold of several hundred clients** who may have had their passwords jeopardised.

Variation: get a hold of (someone)

Get into hot water – to get into trouble

    A. *I heard that Sofia **got into hot water** yesterday.*
    B. *Yes, she left the office for three hours and didn't tell anyone where she was going.*

The speaker **got into hot water** after portions of her speech were found to be plagiarised.

Origin: The reference to 'hot water' dates back to the 16th century. At that time, one way to keep unwelcome guests away was to throw hot water on them!

Variation: be in hot water

Get one's point across – to make something clear to someone

    A. *I don't think anyone in the meeting understood what I was trying to say.*
    B. *Well, maybe there's a better way to **get your point across**.*

Listening to your classmates' points of view first will enable you to **get your point across** without it seeming too harsh.

Get (someone) up to speed – to give someone all the information they need

    A. *Did anything exciting happen in the office while I was away?*
    B. *Let's have lunch today, and I'll **get you up to speed**.*

We'll do our best to **get you up to speed** on the latest Black Friday and Cyber Monday deals.

Variation: up to speed; get up to speed; bring (someone) up to speed

Get the ball rolling – to do something that starts an activity

    A. *I think we're all here now, Ms. Lopez.*
    B. *Great, thanks Kevin. Why don't I **get the ball rolling** by quickly introducing our team?*

If you can't seem to get a sale, there are several things you can do to **get the ball rolling**.

Variation: start the ball rolling; keep the ball rolling

Get the short end of the stick – (US) to suffer the bad effects of a situation

    A. *Were you able to close the deal?*
    B. *Yes, but now I worry that we may have **got the short end of the stick**.*

The Northeast, and its coastal towns in particular, may **get the short end of the stick** in terms of weather conditions.

Variation: pull the short straw

Get to the bottom of something – to find an explanation for something

    A. *Why do you think they rejected our bid? Ours was the most competitive.*
    B. *I have no idea, but I plan to **get to the bottom of it**.*

The reality is that it is very hard for investigators to **get to the bottom of the bullying complaints**.

Give (someone) a hand – to give someone assistance

    A. *If you're not busy, can you **give me a hand** with this spreadsheet?*
    B. *Sure, I'd be happy to help as soon as I finish this email.*

Their major concern was that there was a child still in the car, which is why the police asked other agencies to come and **give them a hand**.

Variation: lend someone a hand

Go overboard – to do something too much

    A. *How many people are you expecting for Kate's retirement party?*
    B. *Only about 20, so I wouldn't **go overboard** on the food.*

The actor is active on social media, but he is careful not to **go overboard** with his posts, like other celebrities do.

Origin: The idiom began as a literal nautical phrase during the 17th century. It took on its figurative meaning in the early 20th century.

Go the extra mile – to do more than what is required

    A. *This is one of my favourite hotels.*
    B. *Mine too. They always **go the extra mile** to make their guests feel welcome.*

Local rescuer **goes the extra mile** to help dogs with special needs find forever homes.

Go through (something) with a fine-toothed comb – to examine something very closely

    A. *Something about these sales projections doesn't feel right.*
    B. *I agree. I think we need to **go through them with a fine-toothed comb**.*

Abigail was advised to **go through the job application with a fine-toothed comb** to see if leadership, initiative or management is required.

Origin: The idiom originated in the mid-18th century and comes from the physical action of using a *fine-toothed comb*. These special combs, with their closely spaced teeth, were often used to comb out lice (a very tiny insect) from a person's hair.

Variation: go over something with a fine-tooth/toothed comb

Go through the roof – to rise to a very high level

    A. *How has your new social media campaign affected sales?*
    B. *I'm still shocked. Sales have **gone through the roof** since we launched.*

With the unseasonably warm weather, sales of garden products and equipment have **gone through the roof**.

Origin: The idiom comes from the early 20th century. If something were to literally go through the roof of a house, it would have had to rise very high and quickly.

Go with the flow – to do what everyone else is doing

    A. *Do you have any advice on how I could fit in here?*
    B. *I'd suggest just listening a lot and **going with the flow** for a while.*

In this new economy, someone who can **go with the flow** and adapt to fluid situations will be more successful than someone who cannot.

Half the battle – a significant part of the work that is needed

    A. *Getting people registered to vote is only **half the battle**.*
    B. *Right. We also need to get them to the polls on Election Day.*

Idiom dictionary

For Australia's animals, avoiding bush fires is only **half the battle**. The hours, days and weeks after a fire bring a whole new set of challenges.

Have a lot on one's plate – to have many things to do

    A. *Are you free to have lunch with me?*
    B. *Not really, sorry. I **have a lot on my plate** this week.*

Rachael Finch **has a lot on her plate**, but being a mum, model and TV presenter doesn't seem to be enough for the entrepreneur who has also started her very own health and beauty brand.

Variation: have enough on one's plate

Have egg on one's face – to appear foolish

    A. *Allie introduced the CEO to her team, but she mispronounced his name.*
    B. *Oh, no! She must have really **had egg on her face**!*

The senator **had egg on his face** after his lies against his opponent were exposed.

Origin: The idiom may derive from the early 20th century, when dissatisfied audience members threw eggs at theatre performers who they were dissatisfied with.

Have money to burn – to have more money than one needs

    A. *Look at these prices! Why would anyone spend €200 on a candle?*
    B. *I guess this boutique caters to people who **have money to burn**.*

Right now, it looks like investors **have money to burn** as they are willing to buy stocks at nearly double price.

Variation: burn through money

Have one's ducks in a row – to be well-prepared for what is going to happen

    A. *Are you ready for your trip to Dubai?*
    B. *Almost. I'm working to **get all my ducks in a row** before I leave.*

When shopping for a new apartment in a community with a limited number of homes, it's especially important to **have your financial ducks in a row** before the launch of sales.

Origin: One theory is that this idiom comes from a popular carnival game in which someone uses an air gun to shoot at plastic or metal ducks in order to win a prize. Another theory is that the idiom comes from nature: a neat line of ducks trails their mother wherever she goes.

Have time to kill – to have a period of time with nothing to do

- A. *Where did you get this perfume?*
- B. *I **had time to kill** before my flight, so I checked out the duty-free stores.*

If you **have time to kill** and you want to see Europe, I think going by Interrail would be fun, but it's not an efficient means of transportation.

Variation: kill time

Hit pay dirt – (US) to make a lot of money quickly

- A. *Did the band struggle for a long time before they became successful?*
- B. *Not at all. They **hit pay dirt** with their very first single.*

JK Rowling **hit pay dirt** with the Harry Potter franchise, and has made millions from publication and licensing deals.

Origin: The idiom comes from the 1850s, during the California Gold Rush. In mining, 'pay dirt' refers to the soil that contains a large amount of a particular mineral. When a gold miner hits pay dirt, they have dug deep enough to find enough gold to make a large profit.

Hit the nail on the head – to describe exactly what's causing a situation or problem

- A. *Alice says that the reason we failed is because we don't truly understand the end-user.*
- B. *I couldn't agree more. She really **hit the nail on the head** with that one.*

Chris really **hit the nail on the head** by stating that what the firm lacks most is empathy.

Origin: The idiom probably has its roots in carpentry. When you hammer a nail, you want to be exact and precise in order to get the desired result.

Hold one's tongue – to stop oneself from speaking

    A. *Why didn't you say anything to Julia when you had the chance?*
    B. *I wanted to, but I decided to **hold my tongue** and wait for a better time.*

When Pedro said his friend's business idea was terrible, some said he should have **held his tongue**, while others admired him for expressing his concerns so openly and honestly.

Variation: bite one's tongue

In a nutshell – in only a few words

    A. *I haven't had a chance to read her business plan yet.*
    B. *Well, **in a nutshell**, she wants a small loan to start a food-truck business.*

The report describes the political party **in a nutshell**: jaw-dropping incompetence and a total disregard for others.

In one ear and out the other – forgotten immediately after being heard

    A. *Did he take your advice?*
    B. *I don't think so. It probably just went **in one ear and out the other**.*

It's as if the instructions Kyle received from the legal department went **in one ear and out the other**, and now the project is in serious trouble.

In the driver's seat – to be in control of a situation

    A. *Do you think the company will improve under the new CEO?*
    B. *Sure. If she**'s in the driver's seat**, I'm confident that things will turn around.*

In housing news, home-sellers **are in the driver's seat** due to high buyer demand.

In the market for something – interested in buying something

    A. *I hear that you're **in the market for a new car**. Is that right?*
    B. *Yes. My old one died last week so I've been looking around.*

If you are **in the market for a lake home** right now, you will probably end up paying over the list price.

Work It Out with Business Idioms

Keep one's cool – to remain calm and not become upset or angry

    A. *Were you nervous during your job interview?*
    B. *Yes! But I tried to **keep my cool** and not let my nervousness show.*

A reporter had a close call when part of a bridge collapsed while she was on location reporting on a massive flood. She **kept her cool**, and, luckily, was able to safely get off the bridge.

Keep one's eye on the prize – to keep one's focus on achieving a goal

    A. *I want to be a doctor, but sometimes all this studying gets me down.*
    B. *I'm sure it's tough. Just remember to **keep your eye on the prize**.*

Carol told them to **keep their eyes on the prize** if they want educational reform to be successful.

Learn the ropes – to learn how to do a task or job

    A. *Are you ready to take over as team leader?*
    B. *I'd be more comfortable if I had more time to **learn the ropes** first.*

This tool can help new traders to quickly fine-tune their strategies and **learn the ropes** of online trading.

Origin: The idiom comes from the world of sailing, where, traditionally, new recruits had to tie knots and move ropes when raising a sail.

Variation: know the ropes

Leave no stone unturned – to do everything one can to achieve a goal

    A. *Do you think the government is doing enough to find out who leaked the information?*
    B. *I do. They've promised to **leave no stone unturned** in their efforts to find the leak.*

The police department will **leave no stone unturned** in its investigation into the disappearance of the local teen.

Origin: The idiom comes from an ancient Greek legend about a general who buried treasure in his tent after a defeat. Those looking for the treasure were advised to turn over *every* stone in their effort to find it.

Make a fast buck – (US) to earn money quickly and easily

    A. *I enjoyed the first movie, but the sequel was very disappointing.*
    B. *I think the movie studio was just trying to **make a fast buck** with this one.*

People who want to **make a fast buck** from the misfortune of others are always looking for their next opportunity.

Variation: make a quick buck

Meet (someone) halfway – to compromise with someone

    A. *Did our overseas partner agree to our latest proposal?*
    B. *Not yet, but we hope we can find a compromise and that they'll **meet us halfway**.*

The new leader hopes to heal the political divisions, but the opposition must **meet him halfway**.

More than meets the eye – more than there appears to be at first

    A. *There is something odd about the way Jessica was fired last week.*
    B. *I agree. I think there's definitely **more than meets the eye** there.*

It may not seem like it at first, but a quality yoga mat certainly delivers **more than meets the eye**.

Variation: more (to something) than meets the eye

No strings attached – having no conditions or expectations on an agreement

    A. *This deal seems too good to be true.*
    B. *I find you should be careful of any offer that claims to have **no strings attached**.*

Corner Bakery is serving anyone who walks through its doors a free cup of coffee, with **no strings attached**.

Origin: The idiom comes from the clothing industry, where a flaw in a piece of fabric would be marked by a string. A tailor who wanted cloth without any flaws would ask for fabric 'with no strings attached'.

Not going to fly – not going to work well

    A. *If you had the chance, would you like to do your job from home?*
    B. *I would, but the idea is **not going to fly** with my boss and team.*

Whereas the idea of universal basic income might be feasible in some countries, it's simply **not going to fly** in the United States.

Variation: won't fly

On the same page – in agreement on how things should be done

    A. *We can't move forward until our supplier fixes the problem.*
    B. *I'm glad to hear that we're **on the same page** on this.*

Keeping your remote team **on the same page** as you and your team members is important if you want a happy, healthy team that is efficient and gets results.

Origin: One theory is that the idiom comes from singing in a choir, where each singer has to be on the same page of music. Another theory is that it comes from meetings or classes, where each member has to refer to the same page in order to understand what is going on.

Variation: singing from the same hymn sheet (UK)

Par for the course – normal, not unusual at all

    A. *I heard that we're not getting a raise again this year.*
    B. *I'm not surprised. That's **par for the course** at this point.*

The restaurant is perhaps Tokyo's worst-kept curry secret. Weekend queues are **par for the course**.

Origin: The idiom comes from golf, where it refers to the number of shots, also known as 'par', that a golfer needs to finish the entire course.

Pull out all the stops – to make every possible effort to achieve something

    A. *I enjoyed Carol's retirement party last night.*
    B. *I did, too. The company really **pulled out all the stops** to make sure it was memorable.*

The singing-competition contestants **pulled out all the stops** for their final performance of the night.

Origin: The idiom refers to the knobs (or 'stops') found on a pipe organ that control its loudness. When these stops are pulled out, the instrument achieves its maximum volume.

Push (someone) over the finish line – to make a final effort towards a goal

    A. *We want to thank the whole team for the long hours you all put in to this project.*
    B. *It was your hard work and dedication that helped* **push us over the finish line**.

A surprising number of rural votes heled **push the candidate over the finish line.**

Variation: push someone over the finishing line

Put (something) into action – to implement a plan or idea

    A. *When do you think you'll be ready?*
    B. *I think we'll need another week to* **put our plan into action.**

The company's next step is to **put these ideas into action.**

Put one's best foot forward – to make the best possible impression

    A. *Do you feel that you're prepared for your job interview?*
    B. *Yes, I think so. I know I really need to* **put my best foot forward** *if I want this job.*

All home sellers want to **put their best foot forward**, and that means doing things like touching up paint and mending broken fixtures.

Put one's cards on the table – to talk openly about one's feelings and intentions

    A. *Why did you tell her that you were thinking of quitting?*
    B. *I just thought now was the time to* **put my cards on the table.**

The prime minister expressed his hope that, in the next negotiating session, both sides will be prepared to **put their cards on the table** so that the best possible deal can be achieved.

Origin: The idiom comes from the card game of poker, where, at the end of each hand, players have to put their cards on the table to prove which is the winning hand.

Variation: lay one's cards on the table

Put (someone) on the spot – to ask someone a question that's difficult to answer

    A. *Your question about the recent drop in sales surprised me.*
    B. *Sorry, but I really didn't mean to **put you on the spot**.*

The talk show host apologised after it was pointed out that her question had **put her guest on the spot**.

Rack one's brains – to think very hard about something

    A. *Did you ever figure out how to solve that problem?*
    B. *I've been **racking my brains** all weekend and I still can't find a solution.*

The young entrepreneur **racked his brains** and came up the idea of selling items made from plastic and other recycled materials.

Variation: rack one's brain

Set one's mind to something – to give something one's complete attention and effort

    A. *I hope I can come up with a good marketing strategy for our new app.*
    B. *I'm sure you can if you **set your mind to it**.*

Lisa's weight-loss journey taught her that, once **she sets her mind to something**, then nothing is impossible.

Variation: set one's mind on something

Set the bar high – to establish a high standard of quality

    A. *Sally has just given a fantastic presentation.*
    B. *I know. She really **set the bar high** for the rest of us.*

Sean Connery **set the bar high** with this portrayal of James Bond.

Origin: The idiom likely comes from the sport of pole vaulting. The challenge increases the higher the bar over which the athletes must jump is raised.

Variation: set the bar low

Step up one's game – to improve one's performance or quality of work

- A. *Paulo lost another of his sales accounts.*
- B. *That's not good. He going to have to **step up his game** if he wants to continue working here.*

With only four contestants left in the competition, they all now need to **step up their game**.

Step up to the plate – to take responsibility for doing something difficult or unpopular

- A. *Why did you agree to take on that account?*
- B. *I felt like I had no choice. No one else was going to **step up to the plate**.*

World leaders need to **step up to the plate** to find a way to address the climate crisis.

Origin: The idiom comes from the American sport of baseball. The batter has to step up to the (home) plate in order to swing at the ball.

Stick one's neck out – to expose oneself to some risk

- A. *I'm surprised that my boss didn't defend me more.*
- B. *He isn't really known for **sticking his neck out** unnecessarily.*

While Brenda cares about the people who are close to her, she is not willing to **stick her neck out** for strangers.

Origin: The idiom's exact origins are unknown, although some ascribe it to the fact that a chicken will stick out its neck when it's on the chopping block.

Strapped for cash – having little or no money at the moment

- A. *Can you lend me €20?*
- B. *Sorry. I would, but I'm a little **strapped for cash** myself right now.*

Consumers are **strapped for cash** this holiday season as more shoppers are looking for the best online deals.

Variation: cash-strapped

Stretch the truth – to say something that's not exactly true (to make a situation seem better)

    A. Do you think it's okay if I **stretch the truth** a little on my CV?
    B. I know some people who do that, but I think it would be a mistake.

Some overly eager sales reps may be willing to **stretch the truth** a bit in order to secure a sale.

Take (something or somewhere) by storm – to quickly become very popular

    A. This new game is so addictive. It's **taking the country by storm**.
    B. It really is. Everyone I know seems to be playing it.

The actress's two dogs are **taking the social media world by storm**.

Take a nosedive – to drop quickly

    A. The euro **took a nosedive** overnight.
    B. And it looks like it could continue to slide.

With a massive cold front moving in overnight, temperatures are expected to **take a nosedive**.

Talk someone's ear off – to talk to someone nonstop for a long time

    A. Have you met Les, the new marketing guy?
    B. I have. He's a nice guy, but he'll really **talk your ear off** if you let him.

Ask any local business owner and they'll **talk your ear off** about insane rents, suffocating red tape, burdensome taxes and a shortage of workers.

The bottom line – the most important fact in a situation

    A. Do you have any advice for me?
    B. Well, **the bottom line** is to always be closing. That's what sales is all about.

The bottom line is that British higher education is continuing to suffer from the loss of international students.

Origin: The idiom initially described the line at the end (bottom) of a financial statement that shows whether a company has made a profit or taken a loss.

The ins and outs – the particular details of a situation

    A. *Do you know how to use a scanner?*
    B. *Yes, but I don't really know **the ins and outs** of how they work.*

Not all of them know **the ins and outs** of Korean culture, and if they're not careful they might find themselves in some embarrassing situations.

Variation: know the ins and outs; learn the ins and outs

Think outside the box – to think in an original or creative way

    A. *Did you like my idea for the ad?*
    B. *You know, I think it's time to **think outside the box** more if we want to appeal to millennials.*

During these difficult times, restaurants need to **think outside the box** if they want to attract customers and retain their business.

Variation: think beyond the box

Throw cold water on something – to be negative about someone's plan or idea

    A. *What did your boss think of your idea?*
    B. *She listened, but she basically **threw cold water on it**.*

Economists have **thrown cold water on the third-quarter GDP expectations.**

Variation: pour cold water on something

Tick all the boxes – to meet all the requirements

    A. *Are you going to take the job offer?*
    B. *I am. It **ticks all the boxes**, so I think it's a good fit for me.*

With its array of cool features, consumers are saying that the new Bluetooth speaker **ticks all the boxes**.

Variation: check all the boxes

To cut a long story short – to explain what happened in a few words

- A. *What happened? Why did the boss call you into her office?*
- B. *Well, **to cut a long story short**, someone filed a complaint against me.*

To cut a long story short, the plan succeeded, and the seller received three offers within 72 hours of the day the property was listed.

Variation: long story short; to make a long story short

Toe the line – to follow the rules without causing trouble

- A. *I heard that you got a warning for leaving work early.*
- B. *Yeah. I think it's best if I just **toe the line** for a while.*

He tells the princess to **toe the line**, to give up on her individualism and accept that the only person that matters is the queen herself.

Origin: The idiom originates from an early form of boxing, where a line was drawn on the ground on which opponents had to keep the toes of one foot during their fight.

Up and running – operating normally

- A. *Is the new printer **up and running** yet?*
- B. *No, but a technician is working on it now.*

It was announced recently that alternate care sites could be **up and running** within two weeks if needed.

Up in the air – undecided or unresolved

- A. *Are you and Miriam going out after work?*
- B. *She might have to work late, so things are a bit **up in the air** at the moment.*

Due to the recent bush fires, Sydney's New Year's Eve firework event remains **up in the air**.

Up to scratch – good enough or up to the required standard (often used in the negative)

    A. *Why aren't we having our annual retreat at the Plaza Hotel?*
    B. *They felt that the hotel wasn't **up to scratch**, so they found a better one.*

The best way to make sure that your website is **up to scratch** is to hire a local web designer to help you.

Variation: up to snuff

Work around the clock – to work all day and all night (to get the job done)

    A. *Has the sales team finished their report?*
    B. *Almost. They've been **working around the clock** to get it done.*

Thousands of customers are without power after the recent freezing weather, but crews are **working around the clock** to restore service.

Variation: round the clock

Download the digital components

Downloadable content:

- Teaching tools
- Handouts
- Idiom dictionary

Download url:

- www.prosperityeducation.net/idiom

Instructions:

- Go to url
- Password: TIAB
- Select the *Work It Out with Business Idioms* book image
- Select content to download

www.ingramcontent.com/pod-product-compliance
Lightning Source LLC
Chambersburg PA
CBHW050717090526
44588CB00014B/2318